D0207699

Gift from the
author

Alf Hackett
2019

DEBATES
AND DOCUMENTS
COLLECTION
MARCH 2019

12

THE FATHER OF EUROPE
THE LIFE AND TIMES OF JEAN MONNET

ORIGINAL DRAFT BY RICHARD MAYNE

NEW AND REVISED TEXT
AND COMPILATION
OF TEXT BY CLIFFORD P. HACKETT

FONDATION
JEAN MONNET
POUR L'EUROPE

THE FATHER OF EUROPE
THE LIFE AND TIMES
OF JEAN MONNET
ORIGINAL DRAFT BY RICHARD MAYNE

NEW AND REVISED TEXT AND COMPILATION OF TEXT
BY CLIFFORD P. HACKETT

Cataloging Information

Hackett, Clifford P.
The Father of Europe, the Life and Times of Jean Monnet/
Clifford P. Hackett
Includes bibliographical references and index

Identifiers: ISBN 978-0-692-19234-4, Jean Monnet Council.
505 Constitution Ave. N. E. Washington DC 20002 USA
Library of Congress Control Number: 2018911012
Subjects: 1. Monnet, Jean 1888-1979 2. Statesmen – Europe –
biography 3. European Union – History.
DDC 940,5092–dc22

Preface

A short, personal (and neglected) biography of Jean Monnet

Jean Monnet, the French 'father of Europe,' had two English aides, François Duchêne and Richard Mayne, both bilingual in French and both working for him about six years but at different times in the 1950s and 1960s. Each eventually aspired to write a biography of Monnet and each succeeded but in different ways. I knew both quite well.

Following is the slightly edited and partial text written by Mayne from 1966 to 1975. When he started writing, Richard had just left Monnet's employ where he had worked, from 1956 to 1958 and from 1962 to 1966. With Monnet, Mayne discussed writing a short, popular sketch from public sources i.e. without any interviews with Monnet or others who knew him. Monnet, who was working already on his own memoirs with collaborator François Fontaine, agreed, apparently without much consideration or later recall.

When Mayne sent his mentor several chapters in 1975, Monnet was very angry, Mayne reported. 'You have betrayed me,' he was told. Mayne referred to the earlier discussion which Monnet then recalled, he quieted but asked Richard not to publish anything until his own memoirs were out. Mayne agreed. The Jean Monnet Mémoires *were published in 1976 three years before his death, and 88 years after his birth.*

Mayne's 524-page text was never published. His London publisher let him keep an advance but told him there was no market for another large text with the Mémoires about to be published. Mayne gave me a copy of his draft text about 1989. Later we discussed a possible reduced, reedited version. We each suggested changes, most to update references and to shorten passages too detailed for readers who already had access to Monnet's own work and to other accounts. But nothing came of our efforts.

The first English biography of Monnet ever published was Duchêne's which appeared to good reviews in 1994 (Jean Monnet: The First Statesman of Interdependence, NY). Duchêne had worked for Monnet from 1953 to 1955 and from 1958 to 1962. Duchêne and Mayne were boyhood friends but neither was initially aware of the other's biographical efforts. When I told Duchêne in 1992 of Mayne's work, he was surprised. He then asked Mayne for a copy and used it occasionally in his own work.

The father of Europe

There are striking differences between the Duchêne and Mayne texts. Duchêne's is much longer and more detailed but impersonal and entirely detached from his own close work over six years with Monnet. Mayne's is an account of Monnet's life and work with frequent personal insights and references to conversations and other interactions with his mentor. Duchêne's biography never mentions his working relations with Monnet nor the many instances where he discussed with him, and with others, writing about his life.

After 1996 Mayne and I both became involved in other matters. His text has rested with me undisturbed ever since although I mentioned its existence in several books and to others who wanted to do a Monnet biography. By then, Mayne had already published several well received books on Europe and other subjects. He also reviewed books and films for many years. He died in 2009.

◄ Speech by Jean Monnet at the first session of the Action Committee for the United States of Europe in January 1956.

Recently another Monnet biographer and scholar, German historian Klaus Schwabe, responded to Mayne references in a book I wrote (Who Wrote the Memoirs of Jean Monnet? NY 2016) to suggest the Mayne manuscript be made available to others. The text below, titled by Mayne as 'The Father of Europe; The Life and Times of Jean Monnet', is a result of that suggestion.

This text is Mayne's but with many deletions and some minor changes in tense and style to reflect the many years of passage since he wrote. It constitutes about 25% of his original work. These changes are based on the editorial authority given me by Mayne. For more information on the history of this text, see the Postscript.

In a few cases I have added clarifying facts or updated references; these are indicated in italics.

Clifford P. Hackett
July, 2018

Abbreviations

ACUSE	Action Committee for the United States of Europe
AFP	Agence France Presse
CDU/CSU	German Christian Democrats
EC	European Community
ECSC	European Coal and Steel Community
EEC	European Economic Community
EFTA	European Free Trade Association
EU	European Union
FJME	Fondation Jean Monnet pour l'Europe [Lausanne]
FRUS	*Foreign Relations of US* (annual)
HMSO	His (Her) Majesty's Stationary Office
JMM	Jean Monnet Memoirs (U.S.ed)
NATO	North Atlantic Treaty Organization
OEEC	Organization for European Economic Cooperation
OECD	Organization for Economic Cooperation and Development
OH	Oral History
SPD	German Social Democrats

Contents

I. Introduction

A grey eminence is emerging from the shadows. When he was in his eighties, almost everyone had heard of Jean Monnet. Honours had come to him: honorary doctorates, half a dozen international prizes, presidential medals and decorations that in Britain would entitle him to be addressed as 'Sir Jean'.

Yet titles meant little to Monnet – not nothing, but little. There were two kinds of people, he once said: those who want to be something and those who want to do something. His choice had always been action.

The action that his name evokes for most people is the uniting of Western Europe. 'Mr Europe' is one of his press nicknames; the 'father of Europe' is another; but he demurred at both. He seldom used metaphors himself. In this case, however, the image is appropriate. Parenthood takes two; and Monnet was the instigator, with Robert Schuman, of the first European Community – the Coal and Steel Community, better known as 'the Schuman Plan,' for the French Foreign Minister who brought to birth what had been Monnet's original idea. That was in 1950. In the same year, Monnet fathered René Pleven's plan for a European Defence Community with an integrated European army but that proved to be premature.

Five years later, Monnet supplied the impetus for the 'relaunching of Europe'– the plan for the Common Market and Euratom. They came to fruition just before General Charles de Gaulle returned to power in France; it was just in time. Through successive crises, Monnet's Europe lived on to survive de Gaulle himself. Three years later after the General's death, Monnet was there to welcome Britain, Denmark and Ireland into the growing Community he had helped to found.

Such is the traditional story. It smacks a little of the pious. 'If a united Europe is created in our time,' wrote historian-journalist Theodore White, 'then Jean Monnet will probably be revered centuries hence as its patron saint.' Perhaps he may. But Monnet is more complex than most saints, or at least most hagiographies. 'Nous ne sommes pas des enfants de chœur.' – roughly, 'we're no angels' is one of his common expressions. His horizons, moreover, stretch well beyond Europe. European unity has never been an end in itself for him; nor is it the only end that he pursued.

Even if Western Europe had never begun to be united, Jean Monnet's part in world events would have earned him a place in history. In two world wars, he made a decisive contribution to the cause of the Allies; in the second, through his parts in the Roosevelt Victory Program and in Lend-Lease, he helped save Britain, speed the liberation of Europe and thereby spare many lives. Between the wars, he was a key figure in the early, hopeful days of the League of Nations, then an international banker and financial adviser to a number of governments.

In the later days of World War II, he contrived to reconcile de Gaulle and General Giraud, preventing discord and likely bloodshed in France. After the war, he played a little-known role in the Marshall Plan that helped restore Europe and did the same for France by initiating the national *Commissariat au Plan*. Along the way, he helped to liquidate the Kreuger match empire, took part in the reconstruction of China and contracted a runaway marriage.

It was characteristic, too, that in the summer of 1940 he persuaded Winston Churchill to make the abortive offer of Anglo-French (or Franco-British) union. From 1914 when he first worked in London and Paris on Allied war supplies, until 1973 when with his help and encouragement Britain finally joined the European Community, Monnet has always been an Anglophile. For several years during World War II, indeed, he was technically a senior British civil servant in Washington with his French passport personally endorsed by Churchill. In the words of Prime Minister Harold Macmillan, Jean Monnet was 'a devoted friend of Britain.'

His astonishing career earned him many tributes. Willy Brandt, the German leader, called him 'a wise counsellor to those in government;' Konrad Adenauer, 'a true man of peace,' Dean Acheson, American diplomat, described him as 'one of the greatest of Frenchmen.' 'No man in the twentieth century' wrote American journalist David Schoenbrun, 'had ever influenced so many governments in Europe, America and Asia.' Another American diplomat, Robert Murphy, although he clashed with Monnet, called him 'in many respects more remarkable than de Gaulle.'

Among Frenchmen, it would be hard to find a greater contrast than that between de Gaulle and Monnet. One senior Frenchman who worked for both at different times summed it up 'With the general, you feel like the least intelligent of men. With Monnet, your intelligence seems to grow.' De Gaulle spoke of himself as an oracle, speaking from within the mystery of solitude; Monnet has always been a man of conversation and totally free discussion, eager to know what other people think. Monnet has little knowledge of any age before his own but a profound sense of time's gradual transformation.

In a world overshadowed by alien 'Anglo-Saxons,' de Gaulle sought greatness for France and for himself as incarnating its legitimate authority. Monnet liked and understood the British and the Americans, and the liking – if not always the understanding – was mutual. He loved France, more than some might imagine but saw its limits and if 'greatness' had any appeal to him, he found it in the civilizing process where nation-states slowly learn to respect rules and institutions, as fellow citizens accept the rules and institutions of their respective countries.

His favourite anthology was Robert Bridge's *The Spirit of Man*; One of his favourite quotations was by the Swiss philosopher Henri Amiel: 'Each man's experience starts again from the beginning. Only institutions grow wiser; they accumulate collective experience and owing to this experience and this wisdom, men subject to the same rules will not see their own nature changing but their behaviour gradually transformed.'

With Monnet, such literary reference was rare. De Gaulle was a discursive artist in words, a great public speaker with a formidable memory for his own marmoreal prose. Monnet always called him, admiringly, *'un grand acteur'* – as distinct from a man of action. He himself confessed 'I can't write but I know how to revise.' He knew he was no public speaker as once he would have liked to be. Action was his medium rather than public words. Throughout his life, at any given moment he pressed for what in the Schuman Declaration of 1950 he called 'immediate action on one limited but decisive point' to change the context of problems which, attacked head on, were insoluble.

This may explain a further contrast between Monnet and de Gaulle. The general, for all his rhetoric, was profoundly pessimistic. At the close of his life he told writer André Malraux 'the question is no longer whether France will save Europe but to understand that the death of Europe threatens the death of France.' Earlier, the words may have been more hopeful, but the music of despair had been the same. 'We came to the door,' continued Malraux. 'The general shook hands, and looked up at the first stars in a great void of sky to the left of the clouds. "For me ", he said "they confirm the insignificance of things."

For Monnet, the stars were there and so was mortality but life was too precious to be dismissed as insignificant. The world was full of problems; men are poor and hungry; violence threatens peace. One man alone cannot change things, nor can one nation; it takes collective effort, and time. The real problem is knowing how to begin and having begun, continue; difficulties and even failure may be helpful, provided we learn from them. To be discouraged is self-centred and pointless when necessity is on our side.

Twice I have seen Monnet shortly after a serious setback. On one occasion, I asked him 'Are you disappointed?' He answered 'I'm never disappointed' – in the most disappointed voice. But on the other occasion, just after de Gaulle vetoed the first British attempt to enter the European Community, I said '*C'est déprimant.*' [depressing] He look up quickly, blinked, then said '*Non, mais c'est attristant*' [sad] and went back to discussing what to do next.

I first met Monnet in the nineteen fifties when he was already no longer young. He had asked me to do some work for him in Paris, and I went to see him with some sense of awe. I knew of his reputation; I knew of his achievements; and in the then small circle of European civil servants, of whom I was one, he was both dreaded and loved. At the High Authority of the European Coal and Steel Community (ECSC) in Luxembourg, where I was working and where he had lately been president, he had been a human dynamo who drove himself and his associates relentlessly. As the train neared Paris, I prepared myself to meet a Napoleonic tycoon.

When I reached Monnet's office at the end of Avenue Foch near the Bois de Boulogne, I was surprised to find it a rather old-fashioned flat with a creaky lift and glass doors covered with lace curtains. Typewriters were clattering, telephones ringing, secretaries trotting to and from. It was all very noisy and crowded. In the midst of it all I looked for Monnet. What I saw was a short, stocky figure with his back to me, in a worn brown overcoat and a rather shabby looking broad brimmed hat. He had just come in and was speaking on the telephone in a dry, quick, slightly husky voice.

'*Très bien* and don't forget the chicken for eight o'clock,' he was saying. Then, picking up the other telephone, 'Get me Adenauer.' He turned around. Under the hat, his face was ruddy, like a weather-beaten autumn apple; his eyebrows were raised, and his brown eyes twinkling; he had a small, clipped grey moustache. He looked slightly Chinese, and very like a French peasant. He came forward. '*Ah, comment ça va?*' His hand, as he took mine, was small and dry. His grip was as friendly and informal as his greeting.

The mixture of domestic details and high politics, I found later, was characteristic. So was the peasant appearance. This is natural, since Monnet comes of solid, prosperous peasant stock. He was born on November 9 1888 in the quiet town of Cognac on the Charente River, almost halfway between Angoulême and the Bay of Biscay.

Cognac is still a quiet town, with rather more than 20,000 inhabitants; quiet and rather dour, predominantly grey and black. The blackness on some of the buildings, especially near the river, is caused by microscopic fungus growing on the walls. The secret of the fungus is alcohol; on whose fumes it thrives. Cognac is the home of brandy, and every other large building in the town is either a warehouse or a still.

Around Cognac lie the vineyards. The brandy-grape area of the Grande Champagne, as Monnet will point out, is no bigger than twenty kilometres by thirty kilometres, yet it produces more than a hundred different species of grape. 'Isn't it clear,' he asks, 'why the French are such individualists?'

Monnet's family were grape-growers. They and the other Charentais have the reputation of being taciturn, slow-speaking, practical people, with a deep reserve of religious feeling, rather Protestant, unflamboyant and tough. Many of them live to a great age. Monnet's paternal grandfather, a farmer who became mayor of Cognac, died at 102, Monnet's mother at 87. In his eighties, Monnet himself looked about 65.

He took care of his health. One of his secretaries has the task of keeping his medical record. A few years ago, she came to the end of a sheet she was using and rather rashly asked Monnet how big a sheet she should start next; putting it plainly, up to what age should she expect to go? Monnet thought for moment, then answered not altogether jokingly, 'Oh, a hundred and fifty.'

Concern with age and health was natural enough in a man of Monnet's years and especially in one who worked himself so hard. Monnet had thought deeply on the subject for a long time; but his final attitude is brisk. A few years ago, on a visit to Bonn, he was discussing old age with the late Chancellor Adenauer. 'I asked him if he would like to live to be 100. He said "Right – it's a deal," Then Erhard came in, and we asked him the same question. He began to tell a long story about there being a cyclical pattern in men's lives. But Adenauer had said: "It's a deal."'

Monnet always kept close to the soil. His work brought him to the city, to Paris, New York, Washington, Algiers, Shanghai; but in every case he managed to live some distance away in the country. Even when president of the Coal and Steel Community's High Authority, he found the miniature city of Luxembourg too urban for him, and took a country house with a view across fields and woods. In his last decades, he worked in Paris but his home was forty minutes drive away in the small village of Houjarray, where he had a stone-floored farmhouse overlooking the fields toward the Forest of Rambouillet.

Houjarray is a quiet and modest place, not unlike a smaller Cognac. Monnet was alarmed some years ago when he heard that actress Brigitte Bardot planned to buy a house in the village. It turned out that she was as determined on privacy as Monnet himself. For the rest, his neighbours were mostly peasants and farmers like his forebears. One of them, some years ago, showed Monnet's peasant qualities.

He was the owner of a field adjoining Monnet's property, and making it a rather awkward shape. The previous owner of Monnet's house, a Swede, had tried to buy the field but its owner had refused to sell. 'As long as I've got this bit of land,' he declared, 'I can say "*merde*" to anyone.' Monnet, too, made an offer but he too was refused. Then he had another idea. He bought a better piece of land elsewhere in the village and offered it in exchange. The bargain was struck instantly. Like had dealt with like.

Every morning, wherever he was, Monnet got up at seven, puts on sturdy brown boots, a thick pair of trousers, a sweater and a scarf, a hat and an old dun-coloured windjacket, and stumped off on a solitary walk. 'Bonjour, Monsieur Monnet,' a woman in a doorway hailed him, or a man working in the fields. Monnet raised his hat or his stick, said good morning and passed on. Sometimes he might stop to talk; he quizzed his neighbours as keenly as heads of state. But for the most part, he walked on, alone for an hour.

Once, this had an unexpected result. Monnet was in London to sign an association agreement with the British. Soon after seven in the morning, he left his hotel as usual, dressed in country clothes for a walk in the park. When he got back an hour later, a new porter had come on duty. 'Just a minute there. Where d'you think you're going?' He could hardly believe this small, tramp-like figure was really a guest of the Hyde Park Hotel.

But Monnet's morning walk is more than a rustic habit. 'It's there that I work' he would say. 'I go over and over the same ideas and the conclusion I reach is generally natural – simple; inevitable. Then I come back. I have breakfast with my wife and I talk things over with her. Then I leave for Paris about 10:15.' There, the same process continues: reflection, discussion, repetition, drafting and redrafting, talk and silence, brooding and arguing, until about eight o'clock at night. In the end, it culminates in action. But by then, innumerable alternative paths will have been explored and proved false.

This process of endless repetition, of mulling over ideas until they become crystal clear or, in Monnet's favorite words, 'natural;' 'simple' and 'direct' may also be a family characteristic. To many French people, trained to be able to articulate complex abstractions and to avoid repetition as a stylistic blemish, Monnet's hammering away at the same point time after time can be disconcerting.

Here persistence and patience count. This too, Monnet owes partly to his upbringing. Grapes grow slowly; cognac takes years to mature. 'When you feel you are on the right road, don't keep asking what other people think. The best way of convincing people is to make your own affair go forward. And for that you have to know how to take your time.'

Time; the very word, in Monnet's pronunciation, – 'taaahm' – carries a weight of connotations. It rings with regret, resignation, stubbornness and ultimate confidence. Change, he knew from experience, will beget change. 'A man climbing a mountain starts with one view of it; as he goes higher the horizon recedes and he sees more. He goes on; and at length, if he looks back, the distance he has come seems astonishing. The great mistake is to limit the future to what one can see from the present – not to realize that, as we go on, things will change and so will we.'

So circumstance alter good resolutions as well as bad. But if change is inevitable and if Monnet is patient over the long haul, in the short term he has always been a beaver. According to Edward Heath, former British prime minister, who had reason to know, 'there are few men in the world more persistent.' He worked incessantly, though not by bureaucratic methods; he preferred a small team, usually a familiar one. For an advocate of change he remained deeply conservative.

One advantage of his team method, was its apparent chaos. In his Paris office one day, Monnet came in to find me ankle deep in filing papers: a cupboard had been emptied and I was looking for a lost letter. I made a face at the mess but Monnet smiled. 'Nothing ever gets done except in disorder.' He was playing the sage; the remark was not even relevant. But it referred to a cherished belief.

This was certainly exemplified when Monnet was president of the Coal and Steel Community – an administrative job he rather disliked. There his task was essentially that of a pacemaker. When he began it, he was already sixty-three but he exhausted people half his age. He set the first meeting on a Sunday and ten days after most Frenchmen would have been on summer holiday. Lights burned at all hours in the office; weekends were interrupted by urgent business. Transatlantic cables were sent at urgent rates to change a word or two in some text. Once Monnet actually summoned his chief aide from the woods outside Luxembourg where the family was enjoying a Sunday picnic.

On another, Monnet himself was to leave on a family holiday; hotel rooms had been booked, seats reserved and baggage packed. But the High Authority was meeting and Monnet insisted on staying until business was dispatched. One by one, urgent messages were passed to him: there were only a few minutes to go before the train left – it had gone and so had the next one. But one by one he brushed them aside; '*finissons nos affaires [Let's finish our business]*,' he said. Finally a crux was reached: '*maintenant je vois clair. [Now I see clearly.]*' The time for action had come.

Action, paradoxically, began almost always with a paper. The huge, Brussels buildings of the European Commission, the Community skyscraper in Luxembourg, the thousands of European civil servants and the years of collective efforts by six, then, nine, twelve, now dozens of governments – all had their origin in a brief document on Monnet's desk. So have many other contributions to history.

Yet, oddly enough, Monnet's own written words were relatively unrevealing. They had the strength of pure spirit, perhaps, but also its deceptive limpidity. Distilled and filtered until they achieved a stark simplicity, Monnet's writings gave no sense of the almost endless struggle that lay behind them – the innumerable drafts, the arguments, the solitary pondering, the last-minute changes, the annotations, the scribbling, the exhausted secretaries, the sheer donkeywork of research.

To those who have gone through the process, every word and comma in the final text had weight and meaning. Fortunately, the anguish of collective drafting is relieved by common sense. Some years ago, Monnet asked one of his staff to propose the rough outline of a preface he had been asked to contribute to a book. 'Nothing could give me greater pleasure,' the draft began. 'Nonsense', said Monnet.' I can think of forty things that would give me greater pleasure.' He recognized both the value and the price of hard work.

Those who worked with Monnet are naturally inclined to exaggerate his place in history. He had the ability, in almost any situation, to convince his colleagues that what he and they were engaged in at the moment was the most important thing in the world that they could possibly be doing. But it can be argued that many of the things attributed to Monnet might have occurred without him; that all he did was give a final fillip to the inevitable.

The argument is made more plausible by the unassuming role that Monnet always adopted. It would be false to describe him as modest. No one could be more self-confident or, once he had thought a problem through, the more convinced that he was right. But he admits mistakes readily; he knows his limitations and, above all, he has no personal political ambitions.

His own work has always been directed toward collective action by others. In the words of Max Kohnstamm, a Dutch colleague, 'an iron rule of those who work for him is, "Never take another fellow's place." People listen to Monnet – and in his last three decades, there wasn't a statesman in the Free World who didn't listen to him – because he wasn't in competition with them; he didn't want anything for himself.'

Asked once by a Paris journalist if he would like to be president of a united Europe, Monnet answered 'No – I'd be no good at it.' Only seldom and rather reluctantly, did he enter the limelight, flattered and gratified, but bright pink and obviously feeling out of place. One result is that his own role in events left little trace in the records. How could it when so much was done by telephone or *tête à tête*? This makes it all the easier for future historians to conclude that Monnet's influence was marginal.

This may be so but certainty is impossible. A closer look at successive episodes in Monnet's life suggest that, for once, the impartial view may be the right one – that nothing, or very much less than what was finally done, might have been done without Monnet's vision, alertness, persistence, hard work, sense of timing and power to persuade.

Seeing his small peasant figure, hunched in an overcoat, travelling across Europe to some discreet rendezvous, closeted with officials baffled by his devastating questions or locked in political argument with a head of government, it still remains hard to believe that this one man touched so many pressure points in this history of our time.

II. Peasant and adventurer

Jean Monnet's career began badly. He went to the local school in Cognac but proved to be what educational experts today would call 'a late developer.' In the 1890s, French education was even more conventional than today. Based on written composition and feats of memory, it was ill-adapted to anyone like Monnet. He struggled on, however, learning the rapid, cursive 'debased copperplate' handwriting that he always used and eventually passing the first part of the *baccalauréat*. But that was that. At sixteen, Monnet's formal education ended. Instead of taking the second part of his *bac*, and going on to a university, like many of his classmates, Monnet was apprenticed to the family business: cognac.

Monnet's father, Jean Gabriel Monnet, would not have agreed with all his son's later ideas. In common with most of his countrymen at that time, he distrusted Germany and he also believed that 'every new idea is bound to be a bad idea.' But he was a man of enterprise. Originally, he had headed a small vine-growers' cooperative that had gone into the brandy business. The big brandy firms, however, were able to pay growers better prices than the cooperative and its members gradually dispersed. As they did, Jean Gabriel bought them out and finally launched the brandy firm that bore his name.

With the aid of shrewd publicity – including yellow giveaway ashtrays which some of Monnet's staff collected – J. G. Monnet cognac was reasonably well known. It would be pleasant to report that it was the best in the world but while this may have been true of the long-aged *Anniversaire* brandy which Monnet gave his friends at Christmas, it can hardly be said of the ordinary, three-star variety. I remember the slightly stoic look that came over Monnet's face when a group of American journalists, who were giving him a lunch in Paris, as a special treat offered him a glass of his own product. Ironically enough, it was also much less 'his own' by that time since Monnet had sold a large part of his holding to a German firm. Cognac was going European too.

In the 1900s, however, the brand name of Monnet was still unfamiliar on the international market where so much brandy was sold. Jean Gabriel trained his two sons, Jean and Gaston, to change that. So it was that in 1906 the young Jean, already self-possessed at 18, set sail first for London [for a brief apprenticeship to master English] and then for Canada, wearing a brand-new bowler hat and guarding a large trunk full of samples.

Canada at that time was a rough country, in behaviour and in language, ready to welcome strangers for what they were, without distinction or rank. The Vancouver railroad was still unfinished. Along it, boom towns like Moose Jaw and Medicine Hat were arising in the wake of the Klondike gold rush–raw, masculine communities of log cabins and frame houses, crowded with fortune-hunters and pioneers. After the Cognac *lycée* it was refreshing. There were no class barriers and no European deference, only matter of fact and good sense.

One day in the Rockies, in Calgary, then a town of 17,000 men and only 800 women, Monnet was looking for a horse and buggy to hire. Seeing a stranger hitching up his horse outside a saloon, he asked him where there was a livery stable. 'Can you ride?' asked the stranger. "Yes' said Monnet. 'All right, then take my horse. When you're through, just hitch it up back here again. It was Monnet's first lesson, he said, in the international pooling of resources.

It was also an early lesson in transatlantic manners. From London and Canada Monnet acquired excellent English with a slight North-American accent. Some people said he knew more English words than French. And when he switched from French to English, a curious change came over him. On the surface, he seemed more at ease, asking much of his companions, losing the hard coolness he sometimes had in French. He would laugh more, becoming more affable and racy; something of the pirate takes command.

The change was almost certainly unconscious but nothing in the two languages as such suffices to explain it. To me, it always seemed like an echo from Monnet's frontier days when this young Gallic salesman had to get along with husky strangers twice his age and sometimes twice his size.

In later days in America, he read crime novels and adopted a saying from one of them: 'Whenever I don't know what to do, I get into trouble.' As a boy, he had briefly wanted to be a boxer. Why? I once asked him. Was it because boxing was a conflict tamed by rules? He seized on the answer immediately; but I could not help feeling that it was too easy. There was a hint of something more aggressive, more rakish, buried deep.

Perhaps it was this that made one senior British civil servant describe him as 'just an adventurer.' In 1940, indeed, to the British diplomat Oliver Harvey, he seemed nothing less than 'a mixture of gangster and conspirator [...] I don't care for him and I don't trust him.'

Change his goals, certainly, and Monnet might almost belong to the twilight world of 'gentlemen of fortune.' Part of his nature even seemed to be fascinated by figures as Ivar Kreuger, the Swedish match 'king' whose partly fraudulent empire Monnet helped to liquidate. But although he used his persuasive wiles to sell an idea or recruit a helper, he never exploited his charm for purely personal gain.

As a salesman in Canada, undoubtedly, Monnet was highly successful. His samples were soon exhausted and the thirsty pioneers called for more. But his greatest success was with the Hudson's Bay Company, originally formed to trade with the northern Indians. It prospered immensely when Canada became British and the territory could be reached from the south.

By the time Monnet arrived in Canada, it had long since lost its monopoly position but it continued to flourish, trading furs and skins. There was a legal ban on selling spirits to the Indians but the company found that brandy lubricated commerce with them. Monnet was able to guarantee supplies. The result was a profitable contract and a lasting link with the company which Monnet later used during World War I to secure a loan covering French government purchases of Canadian wheat.

From Canada, Monnet pushed south into the United States – with no frontier controls, no custom checks, and no need for passports. In North America he said later 'I saw what the expansion of a new country was, what it meant.' It was not unlike what Ernest Bevin, British foreign secretary, was to see twenty years later: '130 million people within one economy, with no tariffs, with an ability among the people to move about without the boundary handicaps that apply to Europe.' The difference was that in Monnet's day, the New World was even newer, the turmoil of progress was immense.

Nor were Monnet's early wanderings confined to London and North America. By the time he was 26, he had already made his way in three continents and many latitudes, from Egypt to Scandinavia as well as the frozen north. Photographs from that epoch show him becoming an elegant, rather saturnine young man, with a dark moustache. He was increasingly a confident citizen of the international business world.

Then came 1914. It was a turning point for Monnet as for Europe. When World War I broke out in August, Monnet was again in London, about to start on yet another trip to America. He had not expected war. His own work had kept him too busy to follow the events leading up to it. Now, he had no idea what might happen. But when he talked with his friends in the City, they were worried. French purchases of raw materials were sending prices up, and there looked like a scramble for scarce supplies.

So Monnet travelled back to Cognac. One his way, in Paris, he heard from the other side what he had heard in London. The British and the French were going to fight as Allies but without a coordinated command structure. Meanwhile, the British were bidding up raw material prices against the French.

Between Paris and Cognac, the roads and trains were crowded with dazed refugees. The government itself was withdrawing to Bordeaux. Monnet's brother, Gaston, a reserve officer, had joined his regiment and Monnet too would have joined the army had he not been rejected as medically unfit – he suffered from nephritis or inflammation of the kidneys. As it was, he had more urgent things to do.

Arriving home, he confronted his father. 'Here are the French and British preparing to fight a war but preparing separately. It's absurd: it's as if they're fighting two different wars.' 'You're wrong,' said his father. 'These things have been settled by those in charge of the affairs of state.'

But Monnet, fresh from North America, was not impressed by titles or official positions. 'Then let's go and explain it to them, whoever's in charge.' Finally, his father agreed. It happened that a local lawyer, Maître Benon, a family friend, knew the French Prime Minister, René Viviani, from when they were both young barristers. Armed with an introduction, Monnet set off for Bordeaux. 'I wanted,' he said later, 'to see the man who could say Yes or No – not someone who prepared documents for somebody else.'

Viviani was a greyish, balding man of 51, a sincere democrat and patriot, a celebrated orator, and already a tragic figure: he had just lost both his sons in the Battle of the Marne. He received the 26-year-old Monnet in his office and listened carefully. Then he said, 'You must explain all that to Millerand.' This was Alexandre Millerand, the rather authoritarian minister of war, recently admitted into the Cabinet. Together Monnet and Viviani went to see him. Millerand in turn sent for his Comptroller-General Mauclère. After further discussion, it was agreed that the unknown brandy salesman should go to London to help coordinate Allied supplies.

In Britain, when the war began, it had been generally expected to last little more than six months. By then, many people thought, Germany's financial reserves would be exhausted. In the age of the gold standard, money loomed even larger than goods.

But for the Allies, physical supplies were vital. In 1913, Britain had imported nearly 53 million tons of goods from overseas, France over 43 million and Italy 18 million. In Britain's case, the biggest single item was food, and especially grain; but no less important were raw materials and munitions. Shipping was Britain's lifeline. It seemed secure with enemy cruisers and warship swept off the seas but it was not.

Between August and December 1914 Britain lost 252,738 tons of shipping to submarines, France 14,414 tons. To face a situation that was to grow more desperate, it was vital to plan and control overseas supplies. This was the role Monnet helped create and then fill.

First, restrictions were placed on non-essential imports. Useful and necessary as this was it could not solve the whole problem because those deprived of imports turned to home producers who in turn competed with essential industries. As long as freight rates remained free, sudden shortages threatened. In the autumn of 1915 the government slowly assumed direct control of most food and raw materials.

The Allies had to organize themselves too. Partly thanks to Monnet's efforts, the first steps were taken in 1914 with an International Commission on Supplies to coordinate all Allied requests and farm them out to manufacturers. But the commission despite its name remained essentially a British organization to buy British goods. This was not enough, said Monnet who wanted to set up joint machinery for all Allied purchases.

In London, such notions were still regarded as heretical but in Paris Monnet had more success. As the months wore one, Viviani had more and more difficultly holding his Cabinet together and in October 1915 he resigned – in effect to change places with Aristide Briand, who had been his minister of Justice. Briand appointed as minister of commerce and industry Etienne Clémentel, a left wing Radical whose earlier interests had been agriculture and wine industries. He was to survive four subsequent cabinet changes, remaining in his post for the rest of the war. Before long, Jean Monnet became Clémentel's *chef de cabinet*, a trusted emissary and a personal friend.

Wheat, nevertheless, was only one of the Allies essential supplies; some way had to be found of balancing demands on shipping against those of raw materials and munitions. During 1915 and 1916, various emergency efforts were made to do so, switching vessels for use by other Allies, for example, when they pressingly requested them. A first attempt to look further ahead was made in the Franco-British Shipping Agreement of December 1916 which required the two countries to exchange monthly statements on ship usage but most of its provisions were piecemeal and unsatisfactory.

As shipping shortages grew more and more desperate in 1917, Monnet argued this point repeatedly: The Wheat Exchange had successfully pooled national responsibilities within its sphere. Why not do the same for the other main commodities? He discussed these ideas at length with Clémentel in Paris and in London with John Beale and Arthur Salter, who was Director of Ship Requisitioning. At a private dinner in October 1917 Monnet and Salter, at the Ministry of Agriculture, saw that the time to act had come.

Monnet returned to Paris and pointed out to Clémentel that France was going to need even more aid during the coming winter, especially in food and that this would be easier to secure through a joint Allied organization taking account of its members' respective resources, losses and need. A few days later, Clémentel came to London for talks with British ministers. Shortly afterwards, joined by Italian representatives, on November 3 1917, they reached a crucial agreement. They agreed to share shipping as needed 'with or without the help of the United States' that had meanwhile entered the war. They further agreed to examine the other hardly less important needs of the Allies.

As Salter wrote afterwards, 'this agreement is not very lucid in its terms. It might mean much or little, according to the interpretations placed upon it.' Clémentel found it very unsatisfactory. He thought, said Monnet, 'in terms of a... finished product. I didn't think... of a finished product because there is no such thing. I thought... of what things can become, as one change brings another. So I said to M. Clémentel, "Don't worry: you have the beginnings of what will follow... not a document... you have the reality."

The reality, as agreed between Monnet and Salter, was that the document 'admitted the principle of pooling the use, not the management of tonnage.' To clarify matters, they supported a further agreement including a crucial balance sheet to show shipping needs and ships available. It now remained to get these principles translated into organization and practice.

Salter prepared a long memorandum summarizing his talks with Monnet and others. It concluded that America should aim to build ships at an increased rate; that it should supplement aid to France and Italy from Britain; that the U.S. should bring neutral and interned ships into service, all toward the goal of transporting and maintaining its army of 500,000 by early summer and one million later in 1917.

The memorandum listed Britain's commitments and asked America to appoint a representative to the shipping board. It also recognized that neither Britain nor America would give such a board final allocation of their respective ships but they should agree to exchange information only possible with such representation.

Armed with this memorandum, Salter joined the British delegation to the Paris conference of the Allies. By luck, on the Channel crossing, he met Lord Reading, a conference principal. When Salter explained his ideas, Reading agreed to present them in Paris. 'I am convinced that what you want is of utmost importance.' Salter's plan was unanimously approved.

Luck had favoured those who were prepared. But Monnet, at about the same time, nearly suffered great ill-luck, as well as great injustice. In Paris, morale was very low. France had suffered great casualties; supplies were short and prospects very dark. Several ministers, as well as the public, tended to blame Britain whose battlefield losses, while great, had not equalled those of France. In this mood, French civilians in London were an obvious target and one minister, Louis Loucheur, eyed them with particular venom.

In November 1917, the 66-year-old Georges Clemenceau became premier with this simple programme: 'I will make war.' In his cabinet, Loucheur was still more prominent. Besides minister of armaments, he acquired the ministry of industrial reconstruction. This clashed with that of Monnet's minister, Etienne Clémentel with Monnet in the middle.

One reason France lacked supplies, Loucheur told Clemenceau, was that 'these people in London, and particularly M. Monnet, are completely incompetent. So he must be recalled. He has never been to the front.' Clemenceau was incensed. He summoned Monnet to Paris. As Monnet told the story later, 'Clemenceau received me very coldly... and said "It is time you went to the front. Before you go, explain to me what you are doing in London." I explained... [the work]... had resulted in an allocation of resources among... countries according to their needs. Then I left.'

'A little later he sent for me again. He handed me a paper. It said I was ordered back to London and start work again. Clemenceau was cruel; he had insisted that paper be signed by all ministers who had said I was partly responsible for the shortages in France. And so I went back to London.'

The closely-knit Allied machinery had been set up only just in time. 'The spectre of famine' wrote Salter in the official history of the war, 'was more terrifying than at any previous period and the cry for more ships to transport food was only one of [...] equally insistent but mutually destructive claims for transport [...] At one period six sugar ships were torpedoed in a few days; [...] sugar in Britain was reduced to ten days' consumption. Disaster was a little more distant but even more serious [...] any one of the current decisions [...] might be the one [...] to bring the crash.'

It would be too much to claim for Monnet all the credit for bringing the Allies to see their supply problems as common problems, and finally to tackle them as a single whole. Arthur Salter, in particular was a main architect of the new system – although without Monnet, his task would certainly have been harder, especially in France. It would likewise be an exaggeration to suggest that the joint Allied machinery was solely responsible for averting disaster – although it helped maintain the vital supply line in the last year of the war.

Despite Monnet's urging, it had taken at least three years to establish joint machinery, even until seven months after April 1917, the disastrous month in which Allied shipping losses peaked. Only well into 1918 was British shipping for French and Italian grain in accordance with the programme of the wheat executive; similar results for munitions came only shortly before the Armistice.

Nevertheless, disaster was indeed averted. By the end of the war, although the Allies had less shipping than a year earlier, their food stocks were much higher. Italy, Belgium and indeed America benefitted from revived British shipping. None of this would have been possible without joint Allied organization. It came too late for a full impact on the Allies' efforts but it came at a crucial moment: and it showed how much more could have been done – and might be done in a future war – by governments earlier prepared to carry out the unsolicited advice of the French brandy salesman fresh from the New World.

III. Banker

The World War had changed Jean Monnet. He had entered it as an amateur; he had emerged as something like a professional. What his profession was still seemed uncertain. Civil servant? Confidential adviser? Go-between? Grey eminence? His wartime role had elements of all four. It had brought him, before he was thirty, into senior inner circles of international officials. It had accustomed him to thinking and acting for governments.

This was not all. Most national officials were trained to serve their own masters and put the interests of their own country first. But Monnet's wartime experience reinforced the effect of his independence which led him to see most national problems as facets of common ones. 'I was struck,' he said later, 'to see how easily Frenchmen, Englishmen, Italians and Americans forgot their nationalities when they worked together to solve a problem.' In wartime, the common interests of the Allies had been paramount. From now on, to seek paramount common interests became Monnet's lifelong habit.

When the war ended, Monnet and Salter, who had worked so hard against so many difficulties to build a joint Allied administration, hoped at first that it could be carried forward into post-war reconstruction. The immediate effect of the November 1918 armistice was to ease the supply situation: submarine warfare ceased and with it the need for convoys; munitions were no longer needed nor were fresh shipments of American troops. But the respite did not last long.

Labour troubles, congestion in the ports, repairs long delayed, new peacetime demands and the needs of reconstruction – all put heavy pressures on supplies and shipping. Monnet, Salter and their colleagues had foreseen this. As early as October 1918, they had urged that the armistice negotiations should place ex-enemy shipping under control of the Allied Maritime Shipping Council.

The proposal was rejected and German ships were not brought into use until March 1919 by which time, in Salter' words, the situation was 'comparable in its actually difficulties [...] to the worst period of the war,' Once the German ships were available, matters steadily improved.

Meanwhile, other problems loomed. Much of Europe had emerged from war devastated, poor and hungry. Many governments had insufficient foreign exchange for life's necessities. The only alternative was to borrow, mainly from the United States. But with hostilities over, the political motive for America to lend was less obvious. 'Normal' financial practices, including 'normal' interest rates once again became the rule.

The real common interests of the Allies now had fewer defenders; short-sighted national interest prevailed by default. What was needed, to prepare the peace much as to wage war, was an Allied organization capable of taking a broader and longer view. Accordingly, Monnet, Salter and colleagues suggested that the maritime council, with membership suitable modified, be converted to a general economic council.

The British government, in November 1918, put this proposal to other Allies. France and Italy readily agreed but in America the scene had changed. Herbert Hoover, who had played a very important part in relief for Belgium, was now in charge of food aid on a wider scale. He liked to work with men of his own choice so he persuaded the U.S. government to press for disbanding the wartime machinery in favour of something new.

Under pressure from Hoover, an Allied Supreme Council of Supply and Relief was established in Paris in January 1919. Its mandate, however, was too narrow to encompass the more general economic problems of the Allies, and its personnel lacked the experience and contacts as those concerned with wartime problems. The next month it was replaced by a supreme economic council, very similar to what Monnet and Salter had first proposed.

The new council brought together at various times in various capacities many very distinguished figures. One eager historian wrote that it 'became for a brief time a kind of world economic government: the greatest experiment ever made in the correlation, control and direction, in time of peace, of international trade and finance.' But it was at least three months late in coming. It was hurriedly and inadequately organized and it gradually ground to a halt after the Versailles Peace Treaty was signed in June 1919.

The new focus was the League of Nations, now established in Geneva under the treaty, for preventing and if necessary settling international disputes. Although the League was the brainchild of American President Woodrow Wilson, the United States Senate refused to ratify the Versailles Treaty, with the result that France and Britain became the dominant powers in what was chiefly a European assembly of nations.

As secretary-general of the new organization, its members appointed Sir Eric Drummond, an able diplomat with an eye for men and a rare capacity for delegating responsibility. His staff was to include former members of the maritime transport executive: Italian professor Attolico, Arthur Salter, and the third, appointed deputy secretary-general, at the age of 31 was Jean Monnet.

A woman journalist who followed League affairs closely described Monnet at that time: 'short, quick, mysterious, with great charm and a sparkle in his brown eyes.' Although his own staff of expert civil servants prepared dossiers for him, he piled them on his desk like a barrier without reading them. He never kept to office hours or administrative routine. Altogether, 'he was even more pragmatic than the British.'

The atmosphere in the League, in those days, was full of hope. As Salter wrote in 1920, 'the need for international action remains and will remain. It may indeed grow until a large part of the government of the world is effected through a world rather than a national machinery.' Although experience gained under pressure of war was no absolute guide to peacetime, there seems to be some lessons that the wartime team could apply to new tasks.

To this end, Monnet pressed successfully for technical committees analogous to those where he had worked during the war: the economic committee, the financial committee, the public health committee, the hygiene committee. 'In reality,' as one commentator put it,' those committees were already the embryo of a European organization.'

One of Monnet's manifold tasks at the League was to assist in partitioning Upper Silesia between Germany and Poland, both of which he persuaded to recognize the tribunal he set up to settle disputes. Another achievement, still more crucial, was his contribution to the reconstruction of Austria. Here defeat had not merely crushed a country; it had toppled and dismembered an empire. Before the war, Austro-Hungary had been the banker of south-eastern Europe and Vienna a glittering capital. Now, with the war three years past, Austria was on the edge of starvation and Vienna a ghost city, crowded with hungry, shuffling refugees.

The whole country seemed unable to produce or earn the necessities of life. Foreign loans temporarily gave relief. Inflation had to stop by stopping the issue of worthless banknotes, by a purge of the administration, by restoring tax revenues and by protecting the country from threatening neighbours, especially Czechoslovakia and Italy. In desperation the country appealed to the League.

But simply giving more money was no help. At this point Monnet had what his friend Salter described as 'a brilliant idea.' conceived during a motor launch ride on Lake Geneva. They had discussed, with a British Treasury official, the bitter political struggle in Vienna between rival political parties. The situation seemed hopeless. But Monnet, with a flash of political genius, said

> "Yes, the situation is indeed desperate. This is our chance.
> For while Austria's neighbours are planning a competitive

scramble, each is probably more anxious that her neighbour should not win than she is to win herself. Here... may be the force... to give a chance to save the country. How can it be used?"

The challenge was to use the crisis to restore Austria to her pre-war affluence which would relieve pressure from her competing neighbours without anyone of them losing. If Austria could again become an area affluent banker her neighbours could relax. Salter and his colleagues worked hard to find a commissioner-general to take charge of the economy and quiet the political chaos.

With characteristic difficulties, efforts of persuasion, last minute hitches and uncertainties, the plan launched that fine Sunday on Lake Geneva was carried out. Monnet, also characteristically, stayed in the background. His task had been to recognize the chance for action and the moment to initiate it; the rest had been the work of experts and statesmen with Monnet's words and character as their spur.

In economic terms, the plan succeeded; in longer political terms the tensions between rival political parties continued the tensions which were one factor in the long train of events that finally led to the *Anschluss* with Germany in 1938.

Monnet's other main concern in this early post-war period, and a further partial failure, was the question of reparations. Winston Churchill later called the whole complex of reparations and war debt settlements, with justice, 'a sad story of complicated idiocy.' But the call for Germany to compensate the victims of aggression seemed logical and just to many at the time. During the war, France, in particular had suffered appalling losses: over 1.4 million dead, 2.8 million wounded and 537,000 captured or missing. Numerically, British losses were slightly fewer, German losses rather greater. But in proportion to her active male population, France had suffered the most.

Northern France and Belgium, moreover, had been devastated by shelling and invasion, whereas German territory was relative unscathed. Finally, the war had seen France invaded by Germany for the second time in little more than a generation. It was not surprising that public opinion in France, even more than in Britain, pressed hard for severe reparation clauses in the Versailles Treaty.

Lloyd George, who despite a few fiery speeches, was in favour of moderation, ensured that no absolute figures were insisted on in the vindictive settlement of 1919. The whole question of how much Germany should pay, and in what form, was left therefore to be settled by the reparations commission set up in Paris.

It was shortly after this that Maynard Keynes, the eminent economist, denounced the whole principle of reparations in his brilliant polemic *The Economic Consequences of the Peace*. A productive German economy, he argued, was essential to the future prosperity of Europe. What was more, if Germany paid reparations in kind she might disrupt her former enemies' industries, while she could only pay in cash either by exporting goods – which other countries resisted – or by raising large and unrepayable loans in the United States – to which the recipients of reparations promptly returned in repayment of their own war debts to America.

Pressure for cash reparations continued unabated by such arguments and the intransigence of the French government was aided by an accident of history. Those who drafted the peace treaty took great care that there was no deadlock in the reparations commission: they made a system where it was always possible to muster an odd number of votes. America's unexpected failure to ratify the treaty threw off the mathematics. There was now always an even number of votes in the commission and deadlock could only be resolved by the president's vote. The president, as previously agreed, was Raymond Poincaré, who until February 1920 was president of France.

It was to Poincaré that Jean Monnet made a third and final appeal to limit the damage to be caused by excessive reparations. Why not, he asked, raise a loan in Europe? Everyone agreed that this would be a possible solution but Poincaré said No. He had no objection in principle to a loan but insisted it should not put a ceiling on reparations. 'When I finished explaining,' Monnet recounted, 'Poincaré said: "You mean to say that German reparations should be limited? No – I will never do that. Reparation is not an economic affair; it is a political pressure." The conversation finished. There was no point in pursuing it any further. But that gives you the picture. He still thought in terms of domination.'

Poincaré's attitude, and the whole spirit of domination that had coloured the Versailles Treaty, were among the things that began to disillusion Monnet about the prospects of the League of Nations. Throughout 1921, Aristide Briand was again prime minister and he sought reconciliation with Germany but in January 1922 he was forced to resign. In his place, Poincaré was appointed and with President Millerand, the two were now free to pursue their cherished intransigence toward Germany.

The sequel is well known. When the Germans requested a reparations moratorium in July, Poincaré thought this an excuse to avoid paying. When coal deliveries failed from Germany the following winter, French troops invaded the Ruhr. The German mark collapsed – under a flood of recklessly printed paper money, which made further nonsense of reparations accounting, enriched a few speculators and, by ruining those Germans who depended on fixed incomes, ultimately helped prepare the way for Adolf Hitler's Nazi revolution.

It was in 1923, shortly after the occupation of the Ruhr, that Monnet resigned from the League. His departure, as one observer put it, caused 'a moment of universal consternation.' Why had he gone?

'We had thought,' Monnet explained later, 'that the governments were moderate and by their moderation and their desire to solve problems, would make some concessions to one another. That's not so. They didn't. They didn't because they had the right of

– what is called – national sovereignty, unrestricted, full – and of saying no to any proposal whether they had any reason or not. Their decision… settled the matter… The world was at peace, the pressure relaxed, and the necessity which we had experienced in the war wasn't there… I realized the system wasn't working, that something else had to be done… Good will was not enough. A certain pressure at certain time was necessary. How to do that was the problem. 'It took me years to understand it.'

'So I left… the future showed that the League could not solve its problems. Germany was a member, and withdrew. Russia was a member and withdrew. There was no obligation and… it doesn't work.'

Even so, it was not disillusion – or not disillusion alone –that caused Monnet to leave Geneva and the League. His family in Cognac had sent a call for help. War had disrupted the brandy business; big firms like Hennessy and Martell were better equipped than J. G. Monnet to survive. What was more, Prohibition was established in the United States. Whether a bane or a blessing for an alert brandy salesman was a moot point but either way it needed careful handling.

So Monnet returned to Cognac, went over the books, sorted out customs problems, appointed salesmen and agents, and himself went on his travels again to restore the family fortunes. Within two years, he had succeeded and he changed his profession once again.

In 1925, in New York, Monnet was offered a partnership in the Blair Foreign Corporation, a merchant bank which had during the war negotiated French and other government loans in the United States. Monnet accepted. As his assistant, he took the 24-year-old French economist, René Pleven whom he had met in Geneva as a young student who had come to look at economic aspects of the League. They were to become associates in adventures to come.

Monnet remained in the banking world until the approach of World War II, longer than in any other phase of his professional life hitherto. For eight years before World War I he had been a brandy salesman; for five years a civil servant in wartime; for four years an international civil servant and for two years a brandy magnate again. But he worked as a banker for thirteen years and this is one essential clue to his character.

Even superficially, Jean Monnet had something of a merchant banker's slightly Edwardian persona, an air of first-class Pullman cars, chauffeur-driven limousines and comfortable, old-fashioned hotels. Despite his taste for country clothes and brown tweed overcoats, his dark-blue city suits were conservative, almost dapper. His shoes shone and his skin was dry and fresh. He spent his rare holidays mainly on the Ile de Ré, not far from Cognac, but he also went to Alpine spas where he endured gruelling treatment to prevent colds – often successfully – and as well, less successfully, to 'improve' his dry, rather husky voice.

On his travels, he could be capricious; he once postponed, at the Gare du Nord, a trip for fear the train might crash. When he planned air travel, his staff usually booked several alternative flights to allow for last-minute delays.

His secretaries, out of old habit as well as affectionate and sometimes irritated respect, usually called him 'Monsieur' and the same rather ceremonious courtesy extended to his informal luncheons in the Avenue Foch office. There a tiny handful of guests would be served by Monnet's chauffeur wearing a waiter's white coat.

Monnet's taste in food were always rather simple. 'If I were condemned to death,' he once told me, 'I'd ask for this as my last meal.' 'This' was a plate of cold tinned sardines, followed or accompanied by French *haricots verts*. At other times, he greatly enjoyed the roast beef and old-world atmosphere of Simpson's in the Strand, a favourite London restaurant. Driving there once in a rather slow taxi, he looked sourly at the modern squalor near Piccadilly Circus. '*C'est horrible, tout* ça' he exclaimed, with distaste and nostalgia in his voice.

Until his mid-sixties, Monnet smoked large Havana cigars. On doctor's orders, he stopped but still kept them for visitors and staff. A sip of rather ordinary red wine and sometimes a touch of brandy were the usually accompaniments to the working lunches. Faced with a long, formal banquet, Monnet suffered and turned bright pink. His preference was always for discreet occasions, where practical decisions could be initiated over good but plain meals well-cooked and served.

Despite his apparent simplicity and his lack of formal higher education, Monnet could hold him own, almost disconcertingly well, with financial and monetary experts. It slightly surprised me to hear him slip into technical jargon, often in his American-accented English: 'swap arrangements,' 'bond issue' or 'line of credit' may suddenly pop up in the midst of a conversation in French. Many of his friends had been merchant bankers themselves and he himself always had a banker's judgment, feel and flair.

Part of his skill lay in his ability to inspire confidence, as well as to know in whom he could place it. Many people, including heads of state and government, came to confide in Monnet as they would in a banker or solicitor who was also a family friend. 'I don't know why,' he once said smiling, with a touch of not quite genuine bewilderment, 'I always say the same thing.' But at least Monnet's visitors knew that their secrets were safe with him, and they knew, too, that any advice he gave would be worth considering, even if they finally ignored it. He was not always right or successful; many of his ventures failed. However, as he pointed out, 'unless you try, you'll never know whether you might not have succeeded.'

During his years as a banker, Monnet found himself involved in many varied projects, with varying degrees of success. He went to Warsaw, for example, in 1928 to prepare a plan to stabilize

Poland's currency and reform her economy, with the aid of private American capital. But the Polish government, a right-wing dictatorship, never carried out the plan.

He was more successful with a similar plan for Rumania and on Wall Street he was very successful indeed. When the Blair Corporation was taken over by Transamerica, a holding company with headquarters in San Francisco, Monnet was made vice president.

But far more important to him, was a meeting that took place at a dinner he gave in Paris in 1929. There he met Mme Silvia de Bondini. She was a painter, dark-haired, vivacious, striking rather than beautiful, and unhappily married with an Italian husband. He had approached Monnet with a proposal that they should become partners in a new bank he was planning in New York. But Monnet had other proposals for partnership – with Silvia de Bondini. Soon afterwards, she left her husband. Five years later, after long and unsuccessful efforts to secure an Italian annulment, Monnet took her to Moscow for a Russian divorce and marriage which lasted 45 years.

On Wall Street, meanwhile, like many others, Monnet made a paper fortune. Then, came the October 1929 great crash. In a few hours, he lost several hundred thousand pounds, possibly a million dollars; he himself forgot the exact figure. At the time, it mattered more to pick up the pieces. As vice president of Transamerica, he began to rake together what could be saved, and to draw some lessons from what had happened.

Studying the way, the crash had come about, he concluded that what was basically wrong was that deposit banks had been allowed to act as investment banks with the result that the public's savings were used for speculation. When the stock market dropped, there were no takers for the banks' paper and depositors asked in vain for their money. He left the bank in a disagreement about future strategy.

But his banking days were not over. In March 1932, the Swedish 'match king,' Ivar Kreuger, shot himself through the heart. It was the end of an astonishing career of financial wizardry, over-ambition, hubris, bluff and fraud. Even Monnet congratulated Kreuger on his negotiating skill in the summer before his suicide. The Swedish government appointed an independent, international committee of experts to investigate Kreuger and Toll. Jean Monnet was a leading member of the committee. Together they faced hundreds of account books, endless correspondence and nineteen hundred personal telegrams. For Monnet, it was a vivid proof of how much one man could accomplish by the power of personal persuasion – and how much harm he could do if he ever misused it.

One further episode in Monnet's banking career in the nineteen-thirties is worth recalling for the light thrown on his character. This is the two years he spent in China in 1933-35. The country was in turmoil when the revolutionary government was taken over when moderates led by General Chiang Kai-Shek triumphed over the radicals.

Communications and transport in the vast country were essential regardless of what party was in power. Communications meant railroads which in turn required foreign capital. In civil war-torn China, this had become very scarce. Monnet was seen by some key people as a foreign expert who might help.

Mayne did not have access to sources showing the important role T.V. Soong played in starting Monnet's brief career in Asia. Soong was a prominent and influential son in the famed Soong family which dominated China in the interwar years and into the post-war collapse of the country into civil war and communist rule. His sister was the wife of Chiang Kai Shek; a brother was prominent in Chinese banking and a brother in law, H.L. Kung, would become finance minister when Chiang precipitously fired T.V. Soong only months after Soong offered Monnet a job in China.

In 1932, Soong, who thought Monnet was still in banking, was seeking a western financial expert and invited him to China. Soong, a graduate of Harvard where he apparently also knew Franklin Roosevelt, had many connections in the West and knew well Ludwig Rajchman, (founder of UNICEF), a Monnet friend from the League of Nations days. Rajchman apparently brought the two men together for a relationship which lasted into the Second World War.

Foreign capital meant, for China, foreign domination. A few corrupt mandarins had made fortunes from railway concession. Since 1898 all loans stipulated that the lenders, not the Chinese, were responsible for administering funds and supervising construction. Equipment had to come from the country the loan came from, often through agents who had negotiated it. In turn they took large bonuses from the revenue of the railway which the Chinese government had guaranteed. For the investors, the situation was fragile and dangerous. Servicing the loans became irregular. The government named a committee of experts who thought U.S. capital, after the market crash there, might be looking for new outlets.

Monnet arrived in 1933. He settled in the French Concession in Shanghai, next to the international settlement. The city always shocked foreigners for the contrast between great wealth and great poverty but what struck Monnet was that the wealthiest banking houses were actually Chinese. Might this not be the key to the financial problems of the railways?

Finding a way to bring the Chinese and foreign capital together in fruitful harmony became his goal. The negotiations were difficult with the Chinese. For a long time, Monnet seemed to be up against a wall of politeness and equivocation. He confided his troubles to a friend who had lived many years in China. 'It's no good trying to understand the Chinese; you never will. Just stick to what you want and make your actions conform with your words.' Monnet took the advice; he still quoted it to those who want to analyse, say, French foreign policy. 'Don't waste your time speculating about what other people really think. Look at what they do. And make up your mind what you want to do and how to get it done.'

At last, Monnet's efforts succeeded. Documents were drawn up for a China Development Finance Corporation and an important loan. He called on the president of the Bank of China for him to sign the formal agreement. The president was very polite – so polite he refused the 'honour' of signing. Once again, Monnet consulted his friend. On his advice, he called twice more before the president would sign. It would have been an insult, it seemed, to do so without demur.

The material purpose of the loan was to complete the Hang-zhou-Ningbo stretch of the Shanghai-Ningbo railway. This was both more difficult and more important than it sounded. It required the first combined rail-highway bridge over a wide river ever built in China. This was achievement enough. Equally significant was the principle of Chinese participation among its underwriters.

'What an extraordinary man M. Monnet is', a Chinese ambassador exclaimed in Paris not long afterwards. 'The British and Americans supply us with huge quantities of equipment and can't get paid for it. M. Monnet gets substantial fees for selling us nothing but ideas.' Chiange Kai-shek himself went one better. 'M. Monnet,' he said, 'there is something Chinese about you.'

Whatever it was, Monnet retained that somewhat Oriental touch throughout his life.

IV. Anglo-American and pioneer

If Jean Monnet seemed Chinese to some Chinese who knew him, this Frenchman also seemed Anglo-American to those who worked with him. Despite his peasant appearance, his Avenue Foch office and his rather old-fashioned courtesy, he sometimes startled French colleagues by being refreshingly 'direct' – a favourite word. His sister was a pillar of the Catholic Church but if Monnet owed any family allegiance to it, his sympathies lay with the radicalism of Pope Jean XXIII. Although he belonged to no political party, he was if anything to the left of centre. While no one is more aware that all men are different and that they seldom change, he believed fundamentally in equality.

Without equality, he insisted there could be no stable relations between nations or human beings. This was one reason, in his view, why change is essential. Without being naïve, moreover, Monnet was a permanent optimist; and this combination of qualities – optimism, acceptance of change, and belief in equality – made him less characteristic of the Old World than of the New.

He had always been attracted by early American history and its ideals; and although no Puritan, he would not have been out of place among its founding fathers. He not only began his working life in England and North America and worked in London during both World Wars, and in America in the interwar years; he also found himself once again in 'Anglo-American' company approaching World War II.

After his success in China, Monnet returned to New York. In mid-September 1935, he went out to Brookville, Long Island, to spend the weekend with his new business partner George Murnane. Also staying in the house was Heinrich Brüning, the former German chancellor, and John Foster Dulles who as a lawyer had also helped wind up the Kreuger affairs. As Monnet later recalled, they were having breakfast 'and I remember very well opening the newspaper and reading the decrees which Hitler had just issued against the Jews. I said to Foster Dulles and Bruening "A man who is capable of doing that will start a war." Because that was subjecting mankind to total discrimination and there were no limits to his actions.'

With war in the offing, it was becoming clear that both France and Britain were dangerously weak, especially in the air. In 1935, Hitler announced creation of the Luftwaffe. Estimates of its strength varied but by late 1937 it was reliably reported to possess a thousand aircraft with speeds of more than 400 kilometres per hour; three hundred were Messerschmidt 109 fighters capable of over 450 kph. France and Britain then had nothing as fast and small prospects of catching up with German production, qualities and reserves. The French Air Force chief of staff told the national defence committee in 1938 'In event of war, our aircraft would be annihilated in two weeks.'

For France and indeed for Britain, the only alternative were the vast resources of the American aircraft industry. In summer 1937, the French air ministry negotiated rights to manufacture Pratt and Whitney engines in France. But this was only a beginning. What was needed was a large and regular supply of airframes and aircraft. In January 1938, President Roosevelt let it known privately that he was willing to help France; later that year Jean Monnet undertook a confidential mission to Washington on behalf of the French government. The American aircraft industry, he found, was very advanced but its output still small.

The first French aircraft order, placed in 1938, was for 100 Curtiss Wright F-16 fighters. A similar British mission at about the same time ordered 400 'Harvard' trainers and 200 bombers. It was something but it was little compared with their needs or American resources. Roosevelt took a personal interest in the matter, receiving Monnet at his Hyde Park, NY residence and asking Henry L. Morgenthau, the Secretary of the Treasury, who coordinated foreign military sales, to smooth his way.

Mayne was apparently not aware of a personal friendship between Monnet and the family of Dwight Morrow, one of his early American friends. Morrow's daughter, Anne Morrow Lindbergh, was the wife of the famous transatlantic flyer, Charles Lindbergh. The couple lived in Europe after the 1933 kidnapping and murder of their child in New Jersey. Lindbergh was widely respected in Nazi Germany as an aviator and had insights into that country's air rearmament. He conversed with Monnet several times and aided his 1938 visit to the US. Anne Lindbergh reported frequent meetings with Monnet in this pre-war period, before her husband became involved in isolationist movements in his American homeland. See the author's A Jean Monnet Chronology, *Wash DC, 2008 86-119 for more details.*

With Morgenthau's backing, Monnet saw officials from the War and Navy departments and visited aircraft factories, some of them still on the secret list. It was obvious, he thought, that if only France would place larger orders, American companies could produce the aircraft she needed. But it was a double race against time: first, because war had only been staved off by the Munich meeting of British and German leaders, and secondly, because of the US Neutrality Act. So long as peace lasted in Europe, aircraft and engines could be delivered. Once France and Britain were at war, an arms embargo would immediately cut supplies. After Munich, Britain thought it wiser not to count on munitions that might never reach them, and they placed very few fresh orders.

Monnet – fortunately for both France and Britain, as well as for America herself – thought otherwise. He was still dissatisfied with the scale of the French and British orders and the limits imposed by the US Neutrality Act. Finally, whatever their potential needs, there were limits to what either ally could afford.

All these considerations pointed to one conclusion. British and French resources must be pooled. President Roosevelt had already suggested to Monnet that Allied purchases be coordinated. Monnet argued now that the two countries draw up a comprehensive balance-sheet of their needs, resources and their American orders.

French Prime Minister Daladier was convinced by his arguments. In September 1939, three weeks after the outbreak of war, he wrote to Neville Chamberlain, the British Prime Minister, a letter for which Monnet was largely responsible. It proposed a top-level meeting to discuss how to coordinate the Allies' resources and how to proceed for a difficult and lengthy war.

Later Daladier flew to Britain for a secret meeting with its leaders, his staff, and Jean Monnet. Officially this was the second meeting of the supreme war council but its main purpose was to discuss munitions production. The talks lasted four hours but Monnet, alone of the French team, joined the British party on its special train back to London.

There he spent a week in talks with ministers and officials. Again and again he made the same point: Allied resources must be pooled. They should establish, as in World War I, strong inter-Allied executive committees to deal with supply, finance and shipping. These proposals drew heavily on Monnet's experiences in London during that war. As happened before, he suggested London as the headquarters. He was soon able to report to Daladier that the British were in broad agreement.

When the British proposed an Anglo-French coordinating committee, crucially its chair was to be neither British nor French but an Allied official, paid jointly and entrusted with leadership, planning and organization. While this was being established, welcome news arrived from Washington: The Senate and the House of Representatives agreed to amend the Neutrality Act and establish a 'cash and carry' system. From now, the Allies could buy American arms for cash and carry them away in their own ships.

This was a big step forward but it made even more clear that Allied purchases might bid against each other for the same supplies as they already had for raw materials. In the United States, in November 1939, the British set up a purchasing commission under Arthur Purvis, an immensely able and energetic Scotsman who had worked on supplies during the first war. The French had merged its own

U.S. agencies into a single mission. It was obvious the two Allied agencies work together. Ultimately an Anglo-French Purchasing Board was established in New York with Purvis as Chairman and Jean-François Bloch-Lainé as French vice chairman.

No less important was the appointment of the 'Allied official' to chair the coordinating committee. Since the committee was to be in London, Daladier felt that its chair should be French. He proposed Monnet for the job. The British agreed almost instantly.

Today the notion of 'supranational', or at the very least, 'extranational' is familiar. In 1939, despite precedents in the League of Nations, it still seemed strange. 'Impossible,' exclaimed some British legal expert; 'this will be the first time since William the Conqueror that any man has stood between God and the King.' But God, as a French official pointed out, was absent from the organigram of the committee. Monnet's was the crucial role.

The machinery was established; the next task was to see that it worked. This was not easy. Purvis and Bloch-Lainé soon had very friendly relations but both had to contend with national authorities trained to work through traditional, bilateral channels. Monnet was forced to insist that the new Allied machinery was to replace, not merely supplement liaison between independent states.

Amid all Monnet's multiple preoccupations, a key question was still American aircraft. Daladier told the American ambassador, William Bullitt, 'this war can be won only if France and Britain possess... absolute domination in the air.' How far could American industry meet their needs? What Daladier wanted, he said, was at least ten thousand planes. Yet for 1940 American factories already had more commitments than they could fulfil. To increase capacity, it would be necessary to persuade American car makers to produce parts of aircraft engines and airframes – an idea Monnet had first mooted the previous year.

To explore these and other possibilities, Monnet's assistant René Pleven flew to New York. With help from U.S. officials and the

French aircraft purchasing commission, they produced a secret report in January 1940. It proposed striking numbers of 8,400 airframes, 11,650 engines and 14,000 propellers in the coming year. Even short of Daladier's request, the goal was very ambitious. But it came with conditions.

The U.S. secretary of state told Ambassador Bullitt that the French and British must first agree on a purchase program. This caused a flurry in Europe. French officials believed a German attack might be delayed until 1941 and that aircraft ordered now might then be obsolete. In Britain, some experts were reluctant to stake so much on only three American prototypes whose performance was unlikely to be improved. Leaders in both countries were deeply worried about the costs.

Daladier's original call for ten thousand aircraft had been an intelligent guess. In the early months of the war, estimates of the enemy's strength varied widely as had forecasts of what the Allies could produce or procure. Monnet, with typical directness, asked the simple question: could a balance sheet not be drawn up?

No sooner was he appointed chairman of the Anglo-French committee than he set about compiling it. When he did it became clear that the question was less simple than it appeared. Working against the clock and sometimes against opposition, Monnet and his staff had to make sense of conflicting and incomplete data. By the end of January, 1940, their balance sheet was ready. Its message was clear and disquieting: Within two months, the enemy would have nearly 15,000 first-line and reserve aircraft, against a combined total of just ten thousand for the Allies. In bombers, enemy superiority was more than two to one. To intercept the bombers, the Allies had only 2,400 fighters, whereas the enemy had one thousand more. He submitted the balance sheet just as the Supreme War Council was to meet the next month.

Both Monnet and Daladier hoped the council would decide to place orders for the 10,000 engines and 5,000 airframes – despite British resistance to the cost involved. Monnet, with a characteristic blend of persistence, careful preparation and Socratic questioning, proceeded. He had seized on a resounding but approximate number and stuck to it in discussions with the experts. He had fostered a sense of urgency by insisting on a deadline. He had made his case unanswerable by producing a balance sheet to substantiate his hunch.

When the decision was finally made, Monnet returned to the details of the purchase. Finally the warning was taken to heart. When the British asked for technical details, the answers reached London the next day. By week's end, the war council approved the plan which Monnet cabled to Purvis. Ironically, he dictated the cable from a sickbed; that week he had succumbed, of all things, to German measles.

For several reasons, the aircraft orders were crucial to the course of the war. First, and most obviously, they were a step toward closing a key gap in defences. No less important, they helped mobilize American resources. Monnet had secured orders for more aircraft than the total strength of the US Army Air Corps. He had paved the way for Lend-Lease and the 'Victory Programme.' Roosevelt's assistant secretary of war, John McCloy, wrote many years later: 'Monnet contributed a good bit toward stretching people's imagination as to what the United States could produce… I can't be sure that this would [have meant] the winning of the war but it would be the saving of many lives.'

But the Anglo-French aircraft orders were important for another reason which only fully emerged after the German *blitzkrieg* and the fall of France in Spring 1940. In mid-June, the first arms cargo left the United States for Britain. Two days later Purvis received a secret telegram from London: France was on the brink of surrender. What would happen now to the Allied orders? The only solution, as he had already suggested to Churchill, was for Britain to take over the orders. This involved a risk since large dollar debts were at stake.

Monnet wasted no time. By nightfall Purvis had authority to take over the orders. Then came news of the French government's resignation and that Marshal Pétain was seeking an armistice. In cold hearts, British and French advisers assigned the contracts to Britain alone. Purvis sat looking at the contracts. His signature would impose on Britain more that 600 million dollars of new debt. His French counterpart also hesitated; the government that he appointed him had fallen. He was about to sign away all France's war assets in the United States.

By the end of 1940, Britain had received at least six Liberator bombers, ten flying boats and 20 Flying Fortresses. By the nature of things vast projects proved over-ambitious, less was delivered and less quickly, than Monnet had hoped.

In the terrible winter nights of 1940-41, when London and other cities were ravaged by the *blitz*, the British learned how much they owed to the US aircraft industry. Few of them knew how much they owed to Monnet.

The success of German arms against France in 1940 motivated Monnet to act in new directions. A French defeat would mean Britain fighting alone against Nazi Germany. A desperate move for a full Anglo-French Union brought Churchill, Charles de Gaulle and many others together briefly, with help from Monnet, toward this unlikely goal. In the end time and the momentum of war brought defeat for France before any such ambitions political move was possible.

Mayne's account of this effort toward union is omitted here, except for his account of the final events of the sad story of British and French efforts to keep France in the war in some way, perhaps by establishing a government in North African exile.

In June 1940, a French warship evacuated a few high officials to Casablanca. On board, among others, were Edouard Daladier, Georges Mandel and Pierre Mendès-France but the full complement was only 29 deputies and one senator; the government… had remained behind. When the refugees reached Morocco, they were put under surveillance. Mandel, Mendès-France, and Jean Zay, all Jewish, were arrested. All but Mendès-France, a future prime minister, were later murdered by Pétain's militia.

The evacuation of the French government had been only a part of Monnet's project. No less important was the proposal for Franco-British union. Talking to an American journalist in 1943, Monnet said 'Think what it would have meant if the political offer of union had succeeded. There would have been no way of going back on it. The course of the war, the course of the world, might have been very different.'

V. Grey eminence

Still living in London, Monnet's immediate problem was how best to go on helping fight the war.

One possibility was to work with General de Gaulle, who was busy trying to form his 'Free French' movement. The two men had first met in June 1940, on de Gaulle's first day in London. They had worked together over the project for Franco-British Union. Each respected the other; de Gaulle was to praise Monnet in war memoirs and Monnet said later, looking back on 1940, 'Only one man in that crisis had the courage to take the decisive step and that was General de Gaulle.'

Monnet knew that the general planned a controversial broadcast from London to the French people on June 18; de Gaulle discussed the plan the previous evening when he dined at Monnet's London flat. He was not broadcasting that day, he explained, because Pétain had not yet officially sought an armistice.

It was an all-male gathering but since Monnet was likely to be late he had asked his wife to receive guests beforehand. When the general, among the first to arrive, gathered at the fireplace with Madame Monnet, she asked 'What are you going to do, general?' 'I came to London, Madame, to save the honour of France.'

It seemed a grandiose ambition. To substantiate it, de Gaulle drew from his pocket the draft text of his proposed broadcast. Meanwhile, had de Gaulle only known it, Monnet's Spanish manservant was in front of the mirror in the entrance hall, making faces at himself in the general's kepi.

Monnet's recollection of the evening was that the general showed less interest in the immediate war effort than in the position of France once the war was over. De Gaulle's attitude had some point: Militarily, the 'Free French' movement could be useful but they could hardly themselves determine the course of the war. If it were lost, there was no acceptable future for anyone. But if the war were won, no doubt with American assistance, it would be vital for France to have shared in the victory – saving France's honour in de Gaulle's characteristic phrase.

Monnet saw the force of this argument but it seemed to him secondary to helping win the war. The French were still gating their humiliation by saying it was all Britain's fault, that Britain had 'deserted' them. A really national movement might someday emerge in the French colonies but meanwhile Britain should avoid anything that might look as if she were using any body of Frenchmen in her own interests.

Using the immense industry of the United States had been Monnet's preoccupation since well before the war started. Now it was even more urgent. Britain stood alone. She had rescued her army at Dunkirk but left behind the bulk of their equipment. New supplies were needed; the civilian population had to be fed; industry had to have raw materials. None was to be had from most of Western Europe and even the Iberian Peninsula seemed unlikely to remain neutral. The empire was rearming and increasing pressure on supplies. Now, more than ever, the United States was the key source of munitions and materials of all kinds. Yet even here there was danger.

On June 23 the same day that he wrote to de Gaulle [*on France's future role in the war*], Monnet warned the British government that it must tell Washington its full supply needs at once for fear that otherwise the U.S. administration's own need would preempt all capacity. Indeed, between May and July 1940, President Roosevelt asked Congress for defence appropriations more than three times the sum requested in his normal 1940 budget.

Once again, action was urgent and existing plans had to be remade. In London, Monnet's coordinating committee could no longer be Anglo-French but its role in procurement was no less important. It was replaced by the North American Supply Committee headed by his colleague Sir Arthur Salter. In the United States, the former French and Anglo-French units ceased to exist, replaced by the British Purchasing Commission still headed by Arthur Purvis.

Now it seemed to Monnet that his most useful place was in America, continuing for Britain the work he had begun for the Allies. 'What I wanted to do,' he said later, 'was to help in creating more capacity for production, more armaments and thus make a direct contribution... if we did win the war all the other difficulties would disappear.'

Monnet went to Churchill with this conviction. 'I said to him "Send me to Washington."' Churchill agreed; he took a pen and endorsed Monnet's passport. A few days later, he sailed for Washington – no longer a French official on Allied business but a Frenchman acting as a British civil servant. It was a moment rich in irony. Only a few weeks earlier, the British security service wanted to control his movements as a potentially dangerous alien.

The America Monnet found himself in summer 1940 made a strange contrast with Europe. Britain was under siege. In much of France and the rest of the continent, enemy troops patrolled streets and countryside. The clear blue skies above the Channel thundered with dogfights in the Battle of Britain. But Washington, in that sweltering, humid summer, was still at peace.

Newspapers reported events in Europe and committees were formed to aid the Allies. Roosevelt and his close advisers were preparing for the struggle to come. Yet for many Americans, 1940 was another year of 'normality,' before whatever deluge threatened. Fearful of policies that might embroil the country in foreign conflicts, influential figures, especially in the Republican party, were urging isolationism and 'America First.' *[including aviator-hero Charles Lindbergh. See above.]*

Only when the internationalist Wendell Willkie won the Republican nomination in that Autumn's presidential election did the mood begin to change. Outwardly, life went on as before. There were still luxuries in the shops; the later flood of wartime civil servants had still to descend on Washington. Industry was still chiefly geared to peacetime needs. And if popular films like "Foreign Correspondent" and "The Great Dictator" looked across the Atlantic, there was still a great distance between them and the realities that Monnet had so lately left.

Yet America had changed since Monnet last saw it in 1939. A new 'Committee to Defend America by Aiding the Allies' was arguing against such isolationists as father Charles E. Coughlin [*and Charles Lindbergh*]. Roosevelt broadened his administration by recruiting two eminent Republicans as secretary of the navy and secretary of war. Slowly the public mood was stiffening. A possible war was becoming real.

A major task for the British purchasing commission, under Arthur Purvis – soon helped by Monnet – was to track conflicting bids for raw materials. At the time there were no fewer than nine separate British missions, representing half a dozen Whitehall departments. But there was clearly a need for formal machinery now that America itself was joining the scramble for supplies. Monnet and Purvis set about reorganizing and restaffing the commission. In October, it was transferred from New York to Washington and in December, at their suggestion, the British government set up a new umbrella organization, the British Supply Council with Purvis as chair and Jean Monnet as 'member at large.'

The immediate task was to make the U.S. administration 'think big' the new watchword in London. 'It is of urgent importance,' Sir Arthur Salter had written, 'to talk big and at once,' Purvis and Monnet needed no persuading that this was so. In August, shortly after Monnet's arrival, Purvis had cabled London that 'to take the initiative it will be necessary that we present to the administration the full picture of Britain's requirements.' But this meant breaking a complex circle compounded of inertia, neutrality, transport difficulties and impending insolvency.

Previous orders from France and Britain had already led to some expansion of American industry; but so long as the United States remained neutral, this expansion was cautious. Only about ten per cent of U.S national income was devoted to new needs arising from the war in Europe. The result was that when Britain placed fresh orders for finished products – mainly aircraft and munitions – their manufacture occupied the very machine tools that had been earmarked for delivery to Britain.

Other Whitehall departments tended to be wary of placing orders on too big a scale. In turn, this meant less incentive for increased U.S. productive capacity. And as America's own defence preparations slowly got underway, its own orders threatened to absorb more of what capacity there was.

Looking at the map of Europe, many Americans could no longer believe that the British Isles could hold out against Hitler; the U.S. service departments were reluctant either to see machine tools exported or to allow factories to equip themselves for producing British-type weapons that the U.S. army had rejected. Purvis was required to clear with the National Defense Advisory Commission any contract for more than $150,000.

These difficulties were compounded by shipping problems. With the Mediterranean closed, Britain's eastern sea routes were now round the Cape of South Africa. Her Western approaches were increasingly threatened by U-boats now based along the continental coastline. In July 1940, sinkings announced by the Admiralty were more than 400,000 tons against only 15,000 in May. No less serious was the looming danger that Britain would run out of dollars to pay for U.S. supplies.

In late Summer 1940, first steps were taken to break this vicious circle. The U.S. ceded fifty overage destroyers to Britain in exchange for air and naval bases between Newfoundland and British Guiana. At the end of October, Washington finally offered to supply some of the British-type army equipment already requested and to top it up with American-type supplies for a further ten British divisions. An ingenious compromise meant that Britain would now help pay for the capacity to produce equipment the United States itself might use later on.

Such moves marked a new beginning. Yet, in the words of the official British history of the war, 'Purvis and Monnet and their fellow workers [...] had great difficulty in persuading not only the United States administration but also some of the British departments – from whom the most intense forward impulse was to be expected – to take the action that would initiate a really serious mobilization of America's war potential.'

To Monnet, in particular, it seemed as if the whole problem was approached from the wrong end. Instead of working out what would be needed to defeat the enemy and to take action to meet that target, too many people were still behaving as in peacetime – reckoning what they could 'realistically' expect to get in appropriations and scaling down their requests to that level. For the United States, still not at war, this was understandable but for Britain, standing alone against the dictators, it might prove fatal.

The only way out of this impasse, Monnet saw, was to apply to a new desperate situation the same simple, drastic remedy that he had used in the early months of the war. To prove to America how much her help was needed, he and Purvis must draw up a balance sheet of Britain's needs and resources and show how far the resources fell short.

In mid-November Purvis went to London to determine:
- the total quantity of armaments Britain would need to defeat the enemy;
- how much of this total British industry could produce in 1941-42;
- the gap to be filled by U.S. munitions.

As before, it took persistence to dig out the figures. Officials in London feared over-ambitious targets and that large orders for one item might lead to shortfalls in another. Purvis pointed out the immense unused U.S. capacity and that tapping it was a political, not a physical problem.

At last Purvis got approximate totals for Britain's needs and resources. But the Ministry of Supply was still unwilling to work out the deficit which they felt might be misleading. Instead Purvis had to do the arithmetic himself. The result was startling – far bigger than anything either government had so far imagined.

Back in Washington, Purvis was anxious to try out the figures on President Roosevelt. Treasury Secretary Henry Morgenthau was present and he later described Purvis's cautious approach. Mr Churchill, he announced would soon give an official estimate of Britain's needs which 'was perhaps of the order of $15,000 million.' [$15 billion] In a quiet voice, Purvis said Britain's needs might be even higher. But to his obvious surprise and relief, Roosevelt 'took this figure in his stride.' A few weeks later, more detailed estimates showed the real deficit was $18,500 million.

'Deficit' was indeed the word. It applied not only to Britain's military needs but also to the dollars to pay for them. Earlier, Britain had spent dollars very sparingly 'as if we were on a desert island' as Purvis put it 'on short rations which we must stretch as far as we can.' The fall of France had put paid to such caution; the takeover of French orders alone doubled British expenditures overnight. To cover costs, there were only a few possibilities: mine and sell more gold from the Commonwealth and increase British exports to the United States. Both these Britain did. But more and more she had to resort to a third expedient: living off her capital by disposing of such overseas assets as the Viscose Corporation, well below its true value. By the end of the war this practice turned Britain from the world's biggest creditor to its biggest debtor.

Soon, Britain's assets were running out fast. In September 1939, she entered the war with 4,500 million dollars in gold and U.S. currency and investments. By late 1940 she had scraped together another $2,000 million from gold and exports but this was less than half of what she had already paid for war supplies. Orders already placed totalled some $10,000 million – five times her remaining assets.

As early as May 1940, Churchill had warned Roosevelt of the trouble to come. Memories of World War I brought a cautionary tale. Then, the United States had loaned Allies dollars to buy American supplies but after the war U.S. tariffs kept out the goods Britain and France needed to sell to pay off war debts. A bolder solution was needed. But with America only slowly awakening to her own danger, and a presidential election in the Autumn, bold action had to wait. 'Nothing before the election' cabled a British Treasury representative from Washington.

During the campaign, neither Roosevelt nor his Republican opponent, Wendell Willkie, mentioned Britain's dollar problem. After Roosevelt was re-elected for an unprecedented third term, he told aide Robert Sherwood 'We must find some way to lease or even lend these goods to the British.' Remembered later, the words had a prophetic ring.

Roosevelt then baffled some British officials by what seemed to them a typical display of patrician panache. He left Washington for a two-week Caribbean cruise on a navy ship. Those who knew Roosevelt well, however, saw that he was 'refuelling'– the necessary prelude to a cardinal decision.

Two events interrupted the intended vacation. One was the shocking death of UK Ambassador Lothian. The other, three days earlier, was a long and eloquent letter from Churchill. In it, he reminded the President that Britain, by defending itself, was buying time for the United States to prepare its own defences. Then he stressed the urgency of dollar finance:

> The moment approaches when we shall no longer be able to pay cash for shipping and other supplies. While we will do our utmost, and shrink from no proper sacrifice [...] I believe you will agree that it would be wrong in principle

and mutually disadvantageous [...] if at the height of this struggle Great Britain were to be divested of all saleable assets, so that after the victory was won with our blood, civilization saved, and the time gained for the United States to be fully armed [...] we should stand stripped to the bone.

The day after Roosevelt returned from the Caribbean cruise, he told a press conference that 'the best immediate defense of the United States is the success of Great Britain defending itself.' He added that 'quite aside from our historic and current interest in the survival of democracy in the world as a whole... it is important from a selfish point of view and of American defense, that we should do everything possible to help the British Empire to defend itself.'

The President added: 'What I'm trying to do is eliminate the dollar sign.' He then produced what proved to be the clinching metaphor:

Suppose my neighbour's house catches fire, and I have a length of garden hose four or five hundred feet away. If he can take my garden hose and connect it up to his hydrant, I may help him put out the fire... I don't say to him before that operation, "Neighbour, my garden hose cost me $15; you have to pay me for it". I don't want $15 – I want my garden hose back after the fire is over.

This was the essence of what became known as Lend-Lease. On January 7 1941 Roosevelt sent Congress a bill to make it possible. Two months later, after passionate public debate, it passed into the statute books with the evocative designation HR 1776. It empowered the President 'to sell, transfer title to, exchange, lease, lend or otherwise dispose of [...] any defense article' to any nation whose defense he deemed vital to the United States. The 'benefit to the United States' might be 'payment or repayment in kind or property [...] which the President deems satisfactory [...]'

The American administrator of Lend-Lease described it as declaring 'the interdependence of the American people with the other freedom-loving people of the world.' Winston Churchill said it was 'the most unselfish and unsordid financial act of any country in all history.' By the war's end in 1945, Lend-Lease was to cost the United States $46 billion of which $30 billion went to the British. 'We may never get the money back,' remarked President Harry Truman, 'but the lives we saved are right here in America.'

It has sometimes been suggested that Jean Monnet invented Lend-Lease. He himself gave the credit to Roosevelt. Monnet indeed played a part in discussions that preceded it. He was on close terms with most of those involved but Lend-Lease itself was a typically Rooseveltian device. It was a way of presenting to Congress what Monnet and many others now could come to see as a necessity.

Yet if initial Lend-Lease deliveries were small, their real significance was that America's vast resources would be on tap. The United States was indeed to become the 'arsenal of democracy'. This phrase, made famous by the President in a radio broadcast in December 1940, had first been used by Monnet in conversation with Felix Frankfurter, the Supreme Court Justice and close adviser to Roosevelt. The phrase encapsulated what Monnet had been arguing since long before World War II. As he said long afterwards:

> I was not impressed solely by the scale of [American] resources. I was impressed by their attachment to liberty. With the Americans… their participation in the war not a question of domination… it was a question essentially of defending liberty… for everybody.

Since the east end of London was first ravaged by a fire-storm bombing in September 1940, London had grown accustomed to almost nightly air-raids – the wail of sirens, the sinister uneven throb of enemy bombers, the cannonade of anti-aircraft guns. Hundreds were killed, thousands made homeless, many lost and buried under the ruins of the slums. Across the Channel, enemy ships and barges were massing for invasion but as winter drew on the RAF held the air battle in check – partly thanks to Monnet's planes – invasion was postponed. Enemy bombers now struck at centres of war production in other cities beginning in November with a massive raid on Coventry.

All this was known in Washington but to be understood it had to be felt. Both Roosevelt and Churchill were outstanding leaders but they had never met. Relations between their governments remained uneasy. The New Dealers around the President were apt to be suspicious of Churchill's aristocratic connections, as of things British in general. Joseph P. Kennedy, the U.S. Ambassador in London, had long predicted Britain would be defeated.

In London, Roosevelt's efforts were greatly valued but there was still no certainty that Britain would not have to fight on alone. Even British officials did not always remember that only Congress could authorize large-scale assistance, let alone declare war. Few realized the battle that Roosevelt still had to fight against lingering isolationism.

To forge new bonds between the two nations and their brilliant, wayward and touchy leaders, the task was entrusted to a frail, crumpled and undistinguished-looking American just turned fifty. His name was Harry Hopkins. In several ways, he was a transatlantic version of Jean Monnet. Like Monnet, he seemed unassuming. One clinical observer, Churchill's physician, Lord Moran, described Hopkins as looking 'like a Methodist minister… his eyelids contracted to a slit that you can just see his eyes moving about as if he was in pain.'

Like Monnet, Hopkins was far from bureaucratic. He had begun life as a welfare counsellor on the lower east side of New York […] and moved on to work with several charities and then to head a relief program set up by Roosevelt. A colleague described his methods: 'While other executives would say "We have this amount of money available and this is how much we can spend," Hopkins would say "This is a good program – it needs to be done – and we will do it.'"

Again like Monnet, Hopkins often worked behind the scenes and knew how to tackle key individuals. Once in the early days of the New Deal, he advised a colleague: 'If you want to get ahead in Washington, don't waste your time trying to cultivate the favour of the men with high-sounding titles. Make friends with the office boys.'

There was an unconventional side to Hopkins that Roosevelt enjoyed. He liked race tracks and poker and nightlife and practical jokes. 'He came to know,' said a European observer, 'precisely when Roosevelt wants to consider affairs of State and when he wanted to escape from the awful consciousness of the presidency.' But what Roosevelt most prized in Hopkins was his equally Monnet-like shrewdness and directness.

When Churchill got to know him he described Hopkins, at 'a great conference where twenty or more of the most important executives were gathered. When the discussion flagged... Harry Hopkins would rap out a deadly question: "Surely, Mr. President, this is the point we have got to settle. Are we going to face it or not?" Faced it always was, and being faced, was conquered.'

In the closing days of 1940, Hopkins asked the President's permission to visit London. At first Roosevelt demurred. But Hopkins persisted. He enlisted support from Felix Frankfurter. The President finally relented. He announced to the press, in early January 1941, that Hopkins was going 'as my personal representative for a very short trip just to maintain... relations between me and the British government.'

As well as being an old colleague of Hopkins, Frankfurter was also a close friend of Jean Monnet; yet despite their similarities, the two had never met. In the words of Hopkins's biographer, 'Monnet was one of the least obtrusive men in Washington... but one of the most determined and most useful. He had the kind of calm, cool reasoning and self-disciplined mind found in Frenchmen.'

When Hopkins' trip was announced, it seemed to Monnet (and to Frankfurter) that the three should meet. He was invited to dinner about whom he should see in London. Monnet's advice was crisp. 'Don't waste your time,' he said, 'with the Ministers of This or That... Concentrate on Churchill. Churchill is the British War Cabinet and no one else matters.' After a while, Hopkins grew tired of hearing about 'this almighty Churchill. I suppose Churchill is convinced that he's the greatest man in the world.'

'No,' said Monnet, in effect. 'But he is a great man, as well as a great orator. And he is very British. He distrusts theories. He's very practical. He likes to get to the point.'

Hopkins remained unconvinced. 'Harry,' exclaimed Frankfurter, 'if you'd going to London with that chip on your shoulder... you may as well cancel your passage now.'

As [later British ambassador] Sir Arthur Frank said, Monnet had 'realized that... the first meeting between Hopkins and Churchill... would be of immense importance and he took a great deal of trouble with immense skill, in making Hopkins combustible with a fire that could seize him as soon as he saw Churchill.'

Thus primed, Hopkins took the Clipper via Lisbon to London. The U.S. *chargé d'affaires* contrasted him with earlier American envoys who wanted to know if the British really needed all they were asking for. 'Hopkins wanted to find out if they were asking for enough... He made me feel that the first real assurance of hope had at last come; he acted on the British like a galvanic needle.'

True to his habits and to Monnet's advice, when Hopkins met Churchill he spoke bluntly;

I told him there was a feeling in some quarters that he, Churchill, did not like America, Americans or Roosevelt. He denied this vigorously and sent for a secretary to show me a telegram he had sent to the President immediately after his re-election, expressing his delight. I told him of my mission – he seemed pleased – and several times assured me that he was to make every detail… available to me and hoped I would not leave England until I was fully satisfied of the exact state of England's mind and of the urgent necessity of the exact material assistance required to win the war.

After a weekend with Churchill, Hopkins reported to Roosevelt:

The people here are amazing from Churchill down and if courage alone can win, the result will be inevitable but they need our help desperately. And I am sure you will permit nothing to stand in the way. Churchill is the government […] he controls the grand strategy and often the details […] I cannot emphasize too strongly that he is the one and only person over here with whom you need to have a full meeting of minds.

Churchill, for his part, was equally impressed with Hopkins. As he cabled to Roosevelt, 'I am most grateful to you for sending so remarkable an envoy.' In all, Hopkins spent six weeks in Britain. At a final meeting with Churchill in Glasgow, Hopkins, according to Lord Moran, said what he would tell the President. 'I am going to quote one verse from that Book of Books: "Whither thou goest, I will go; where thou lodgest, I will lodge; thy people shall be my people and thy God my God." Then he added very quietly. "Even to the end." 'I was surprised to find the P.M. in tears. He knew what it meant.'

Despite improved military and political cooperation with America, the British situation against Nazi Germany continued to deteriorate. Both London and Washington seemed to understand the ultimate need for America's entry in the war but the political situation for Roosevelt was no clearer. Monnet recognized, in his first year in the United States, that his first task was to speed up American supplies. 'I had one essential preoccupation when I was in Washington,' he later recalled, 'that was that more armaments, more planes, would win the war.'

In the words of the official war history, 'British policy in Washington, formulated in large measure by Monnet's planning mind and propagated by the persistence and persuasiveness of Purvis, made demands upon American industry that were far in advance of contemporary American opinion.'

In December 1940, Purvis had told Roosevelt that Britain's American supply needs would amount to some $15 billion. The President acquiesced in Purvis' balance sheet estimates but it was another matter to turn them into planes, tanks and guns. In this task, Monnet's contact with Harry Hopkins was to prove crucial.

Lord Halifax, newly arrived as British ambassador, soon had a long discussion with Monnet and Purvis, going over what had to be done to secure production as soon as Lend-Lease became law. They had all agreed that it was vital, as Halifax reported to Churchill, that 'the stuff must be produced by the time required in the quantities shown in the list.' He asked the Prime Minister to make this point to Hopkins, then still in Britain. As soon as he was back in Washington, Monnet got in touch with him. It was the first of many such councils of war.

'It wasn't very long,' said John McCloy, Roosevelt's assistant secretary of war, 'before Monnet and Hopkins were buddies.' Nor, given their respective characters, was it very surprising. 'Roosevelt, whenever I saw him,' said Monnet, looking back, 'exposed his views in very general terms. He was incomplete. It always needed to be articulated to realities and this Hopkins did.'

The obstacles were many but Hopkins strengths were amazing to observers. His power derived from Roosevelt but the sheer energy came from Hopkins, ill and in pain as he often was. His insights and scope were infinite, the activity frenetic. His biographer, Robert Sherwood, nicknamed Hopkins 'the Generalissimo of the Needle Brigade.'

His troops were lively former New Dealers who were losing their suspicions of business people as they found industrialists ready to meet their production challenges. Sherwood added, 'One adviser who remained in the background but who exerted considerable influence was the Frenchman, Jean Monnet. He was no New Dealer… Monnet was the great, single-minded apostle of all-out production, preaching the doctrine that ten thousand tanks too many are far preferable to one tank too few.'

Yet despite ceaseless efforts by Monnet and his colleagues in Washington, further down the line a peacetime mentality was still entrenched. Many of the middle-rank military and civil service officers working on supplies had been trained to be cautious. As late as July 1941, as Monnet pointed out in a letter to London, America was still pursuing 'immediate and limited supply objectives.' American rearmament was determined by these objectives, not by the strength of the Axis powers.

How could this be remedied – short of a U.S. declaration of war? The only way, in Monnet's view, was to expose the facts. How much were Britain and America actually producing? Monnet suspected that in America's case it was a great deal less than was generally assumed. How much would Britain and America have to increase production to win the war? To find the answers meant applying the Monnet and Purvis balance-sheet technique not just to Britain's needs and resources but jointly to the Commonwealth and the United States.

Suddenly, fate and Germany's biggest battleship, the Bismarck, came into play. The German ship sank a British cruiser and damaged a battleship in the Denmark Strait. Then it made off across the Atlantic heading straight into the Atlantic convoy route. Did Hitler plan to intimidate America by sinking a convoy as he had already sunk an American merchant ship, the Robin Moor? After a dramatic mid-ocean battle, the Bismarck was sunk. This British victory gave President Roosevelt an occasion to proclaim 'an unlimited national emergency' to ensure delivery of vital supplies to Britain.

A few days later, Monnet talked with the Lend-Lease executive director who was Hopkins' right hand man and who agreed with Monnet that any deficiency of production required to overtake the enemy by 1942 must come from War and Navy appropriations, not from Lend-Lease.

By this time, Hitler had invaded the Soviet Union. War secretary Henry Stimson wrote the president immediately that 'Germany's action [means] the door is opened wide for you to lead directly toward winning the battle of the North Atlantic.' But subsequent Russian calls on U.S. production increased further the 'deficiency' Monnet had so long stressed. Necessity, his truest ally, was at work again. Within a month, Roosevelt called for a large increase in tank production as the first Soviet requirements arrived 'with the only limiting factor [...] the ability of American industry to produce.'

August 1941 was in several respects a portentous month. On August 9, Churchill and Roosevelt began their seaborne 'Atlantic Conference' outside Argentia, Newfoundland. A British official who talked with Purvis in London after the conference found him 'full of excitement.' The time had come, he said, to get from Roosevelt the 'greatest directive' yet at least putting all U.S. production on a wartime basis. The very next day, disaster struck at Prestwick, Scotland when Purvis's return flight to Washington crashed. He was killed. More than 30 years later, Jean Monnet still frowned with pain when he spoke of Purvis' death. It was one of many wartime disasters involving air travel: General Sikorski of Poland, poet-pilot Antoine de Saint-Exupéry, musician Glenn Miller, actor Leslie Howard. Purvis was not as famous as these but he was a great man and trusted friend.

On August 19 Monnet prepared in Washington, for Lord Beaverbrook, the minister of supply an analysis of production figures. It proposed that American output for the second half of 1942 should meet the original production targets for the first half of 1943. Both sides were now ready for an Anglo-American conference to draw up the Victory Programme of joint long-term needs. On August 22 Monnet called London to say Roosevelt approved the idea and the necessary orders. The President proposed a London conference on September 15, just before Beaverbrook and U.S. envoy Averell Harriman were to go to Moscow [now an ally after Hitler's June 1941 invasion].

By December, Donald Nelson, head of the American supply and priorities board, had on his desk the final feasibility report on the Victory Programme. Its total estimated cost, over the next two years, was $150 billion – twice the entire U.S. budget as it then stood. Monnet had concluded earlier that when the British, American and Russian needs were totalled they would exceed the entire productive capacity of Britain and America. 'At that stage, it will be necessary,' he wrote, 'to decide on the highest grounds of strategy which requirements must be cut.' With the war still in balance, his words were ominous.

The Japanese Government took the decision out of the Allies' hands. For weeks it had been making belligerent noises. Now, although still negotiating with the United States, its leader, General Tojo, decided to attack. On December 7, aircraft of the Japanese fleet stole out of the morning mists above the Pacific to bombard American warships at their Pearl Harbor base in Hawaii. Within an hour, seven of eight battleships there were out of action. This left two battleships against Japan's ten. The Japanese then attacked Malay, Hong Kong, Guam, the Philippines, Wake Island, Midway, Borneo, Thailand, the Dutch East Indies. They sank the British Battleship Prince of Wales and cruiser Repulse.

Yet within the disaster, salvation itself was concealed. The dawn attack on Pearl Harbor started at 1 pm Washington time. That afternoon, Churchill phoned Roosevelt from Chequers where he had heard the news by radio. Roosevelt told him "We are all in the same boat now."

The next day, the president told Congress: 'Hostilities exist. There is no blinking at the fact that our people, our territory and our interests are in grave danger.' Thirty-three minutes after he finished speaking Congress declared war with one dissenting vote. On December 11 Hitler and Mussolini formally declared war on the United States. Enemy onslaught was forging the grand alliance. Churchill later commented 'We had won after all.' The next day he left for Washington aboard HMS Duke of York.

The role of Lend-Lease, temporarily suspended, provoked British fears that supplies might be diverted to the Pacific. To settle such vital issues Roosevelt, Hopkins, Beaverbrook, Monnet and other staff members held a series of meetings in parallel with top-level strategic talks. Before them was the revised joint 'balance-sheet.' Monnet already had the British supply council's statisticians start regularly to update it.

For 1942, the targets had seemed ambitious; but Monnet had already gone further by December 10. He argued that 'United States production schedules [that year] [...] should be capable of at least a fifty percent increase.' Early in January Franklin Roosevelt drove to Capitol Hill to deliver the annual state of the union message. The entire assembly rose to applaud as he hobbled in on the arm of aide General Edwin Watson. His face unusually 'sharp and stern', an observer said. He denounced the Axis dictators in a phrase suggested by Robert Sherwood: 'The militarists of Berlin and Tokyo started this war but the massed, angered forces of common humanity will finish it.'

The Allied Victory Programme was the work of many hands and brains. Arthur Purvis, Harry Hopkins, Lord Beaverbrook, Henry Stimson, Roosevelt himself, Winston Churchill, Sir Arthur Salter – all these and many others less prominent but no less devoted must be counted among its artisans. But Jean Monnet had always been its most constant, single-minded and effective advocate. Ever since 1938 when he first negotiated for U.S. aircraft for France, he had firmly grasped one simple and essential point: The resources of the New World must be brought to redress the wrongs of the Old.

With the Victory Programme now agreed, it was urgently necessary to set up machinery better able to carry it out. Monnet had been brooding on this problem for many weeks in late 1941. Shortly after the attack on Pearl Harbor, he discussed it at length with Felix Frankfurter. They agreed that in mobilizing for war the United States had much to learn from the French and British experience; and this seemed so important it deserved the President's personal attention.

True to his habits, Monnet had drafted a note on the subject; but he hesitated to send it to Roosevelt himself. Frankfurter, on the other hand, was American and in constant touch with the President. A year earlier, he had acted as intermediary for a Monnet memorandum. He had even sent the President a note from Monnet's small step-daughter, Anne, enclosing ten dimes ('it is very little but it is all I have') for the Infantile Paralysis Fund. A note from Frankfurter now might be the best way to proceed. Would Frankfurter care to redraft Monnet's paper and send it on its way?

Frankfurter's memorandum, only summarized here, started with the decisive shift with the U.S. entrance into the war bringing with it immense resources and manpower. Final victory depends on the speed with which these strengths actually appear. The example of Britain and France shows how a lack of a definite goal and slowness in their war administration must be avoided.

The agencies dealing with production are many but each was under a different authority with none responsible for the over-all objective. Someone capable of acting for the President must see the Victory Program carried out. As Monnet was to point out later in reflecting on these wartime experiences, 'where each country dealt with its own 'part of the problem' there were no common institutions for the main objective'.

A few days after the President saw the memorandum, Monnet wrote to the head of the Office of Production Management (OPM). For each commodity in short supply, he suggested, there should be 'one central statement continuously kept up to date by information supplied by each government.' There should be 'one single organization centralizing this information' and simultaneously receiving the Allied requirements. Such a central office was soon established within OPM.

In late December, Lord Beaverbrook proposed Harry Hopkins take over as supreme supplies commander, comparable to that for strategy. But Hopkins was not only ill; he was also unacceptable to many segments of American opinion. What was more, both military branches opposed civilian control of their weapons production. Robert Sherwood wrote later that 'the formation of the Munitions Assignment Board provoked more heated argument than any other topic at the Arcadia Conference.'

A related problem was that any change in one production programme affected the others. Maximum efficiency could only come if there were a common production policy. This meant a Combined Production Board covering British and American output. In the words of the British official history, 'The first move toward the combined board came in February 1942 from the British Supply Council [...] with Monnet as the prime mover.'

It was the administrative embodiment of Monnet's 'balance-sheet' method. The recognition of necessary forward planning, joint action and common institution had replaced habit and tradition as guides to the provisioning of war.

The father of Europe

***

Monnet remained in Washington into 1943 working the same way at the same problems with the same tireless persistence. By then he had been able to see most of his efforts bear fruit. With his own country defeated, he had gone to work for her British ally and had helped tap the huge resources of the United States. As in World War I, he had laboured in the shadows to create a new kind of international teamwork, persuading those who laboured with him to ignore each other's accents and even each other's citizenship in a common cause.

'M. Monnet', economist John Maynard Keynes said, 'shortened the war by a year.'

VI. Frenchman

However 'Anglo-American' Jean Monnet may sometimes seemed, and however well he got on with Americans in particular, he remained very French.

Although he spoke English fluently, his accent was still unmistakably French. So was his style. He shook hands on parting as well as on meeting. He kept his wrists on the table, politely, at meal times. He ate salad with his cheese.

Although he often criticized French colleagues for being 'too logical' or 'too intellectual', he was cool and logical himself. He was French in his concern to be clear or 'direct' as he called it; in a slight tendency to moralize, in a strong awareness of nuance in personal relations. He was subtle, patient, and realistic; but although he believed in gradual progress – in 'changing the conditions;' of a problem rather than attacking it bull-headedly – he also believed in defining his goals well in advance.

He never believed that uniting Europe or working in partnership with America could somehow change the nature of his country; he was far too sure of it for that. Was it mere coincidence that when his only child, a daughter, was born he named her Marianne?

Monnet had true French *pudeur* [shyness] about showing his deepest feelings; but what they were after the fall of France can easily be imagined. It was natural that in June 1940 he should plead with the British government to throw its fighter aircraft into the battle for France. True, after the failure of his proposal for Franco-British union, Monnet turned quickly to the task in hand, parted from de Gaulle and worked as a British official in America; but, throughout his years in Washington, his thoughts were often with his fellow-countrymen in France.

One proof of his continuing concern for them was an earlier memorandum he drew up in Washington in fall 1940, not long after President Roosevelt's re-election for a third term. Again, he gave it in confidence to Felix Frankfurter to bring it to Roosevelt's attention. Frankfurter passed it on with a covering note, describing but not naming Monnet. The memorandum outlined Monnet's worries about France under German occupation.

France, Monnet wrote, is resisting German efforts to impose a new 'European Order' and to give up her North African bases and her fleet. France resists both because of British resistance but also because she trusts in America. The President should, in his next public statement, show he understands and supports French hopes.

In his next 'fireside chat', the President did not directly respond to Frankfurter's note or Monnet memorandum but used the latter's earlier phrase, 'arsenal of democracy' to describe the American role of supporting opposition to Nazi Germany's European goals.

Two points in Monnet memorandum were also pointers for the future. First, his rejection of a 'United Europe' brought about by coercion, fear and terror and, secondly his emphasis on North Africa. The reference to Europe was to acquire its full significance ten years later when Monnet proposed a genuine United Europe based on equality, agreement and hope. The reference to North Africa presaged a more immediate role for Monnet in the North-African genesis of a provisional government for France.

Late the next year, in the afternoon of November 7 1942, a vast convoy was seen steaming eastward through the Mediterranean, apparently bound for Malta. But as night fell, it unexpectedly turned south. At 1 am on November 8, the first of 110,000 British and American troops began their amphibious assault on Moroccan and Algerian beaches. 'Operation Torch' had begun.

The military commander was General Dwight D. Eisenhower but even he could not eliminate all mistakes. The shortage of shipping had limited the forces available; some weapons promised local insurgents never arrived; one task force landed on the wrong beach. Worse, local officials were far more loyal to Marshal Pétain, the leader of occupied France, than anyone expected. One reason was political mismanagement by the Allies who had not forewarned Charles de Gaulle of 'Torch' nor invited him to take part.

From Washington, Jean Monnet watched events in North Africa with an anxious eye. The dangers were very evident. Whatever the ambitions and respective merits of General Henri Giraud, an escaped prisoner of the Germans whom the Allies hoped could unite the French factions and General de Gaulle, who saw himself as leader of all French Resistance, it would be disastrous, Monnet thought, if Frenchmen were to turn against Frenchmen and the country torn by civil war.

From March to October 1943, Jean Monnet worked to avoid such an outcome. He went in Algiers at the request of the Roosevelt administration in a job he himself proposed with the help of Harry Hopkins. His goal was to seek unity among French resistance leaders.

His priority was winning the war; how to get French support for that effort was all that mattered. His complicated relations with General de Gaulle were involved with the Roosevelt side firmly opposed to the general's growing role in the resistance. Monnet's mission, some in Washington thought, was to block the general. They were ultimately disappointed.

Mayne's long account of the Algiers mission of Monnet is omitted except for the following highlights illustrating his role and taken from his original text:

♦ In the weeks following the Allied landings, Monnet had long discussions on the subject with his Washington friends, and in particular with Frankfurter and Hopkins. To them, in late December 1942, he sent a paper which summed up the conclusions they had provisionally reached. It was impossible, Monnet argued, to go back on what had already been done by the military in North Africa. The Allies' lines of communications must be kept safe. What had to be done now was to make the best of things and build up a new French army to take part in the Liberation of France.

◆ Turning to political problems, Monnet went on:
The sovereignty of France rests with the French people. Only its expression has been suspended by German occupation [...] No French political authority can exist [...] outside of France. It is the duty of the United States and Great Britain to preserve for the people of France the right [...] to determine for themselves what government they will have.

◆ [Another] section of Monnet's paper dealt with the problem of the North African authorities on the spot. Their role, he argued, was... to remain accountable to the future French Government. He was anxious, in the detailed memo, to guard against two parallel dangers: One was that Admiral Darlan, [the local French political authority] or any other Frenchman, might work his way into power undemocratically. The other was that the United States might establish in North Africa, and perhaps later in France itself, an Anglo-American civil administration... Either of these eventualities might pre-empt the French people's right to decide its future for themselves.

◆ These problems Monnet was to grapple with personally and far sooner than he then knew. But he had settled in his own mind some of the fundamental issues... The French people – not Darlan, not de Gaulle, not Giraud – must decide on France's future government.

◆ Despite the Anglo-American alliance, the Allies still tended to treat the French political problem in terms of personalities; this tendency continued when Churchill and Roosevelt met at the Casablanca conference in January 1943. Even with the temporary truce between Generals de Gaulle and Giraud at the conference,

Monnet saw from Washington the dangers of bitter intra-French rivalry. Yet in fact Monnet was now on the brink of playing a far more active role in the French North Africa.

◆ Roosevelt had sent a cable from Casablanca to Cordell Hull, his secretary of state, suggesting Monnet might play a useful role as a civilian to guide the bickering generals. Hull opposed the idea which had apparently come from Harry Hopkins. The latter persevered. In March Monnet left on a mission ostensibly to manage U.S. munitions for the French troops in North Africa. In fact, the American government hoped he could give solid political support to the politically inexperienced General Giraud and thus thwart his rival, General de Gaulle.

◆ To Giraud, at their first meeting, Jean Monnet was:
A man about 50, short, vigorous, unassuming in appearance and behaviour, although well-groomed and wearing a well-cut suit […]. His eyes were bright, his wit subtle, his words prudent. He has his own idea; he follows it. He won't reveal what it is. Every problem leads him to many subordinate clauses, circumlocutions, repetition and digressions, rather than a clear and simple statement. From the first moment I felt that he was a man of substance and that he wanted a place in the French adventure.

◆ Giraud was persuaded to give a public commitment to independence from the Vichy government ruling part of France under German direction. Monnet wrote the first draft. Giraud's goal, he admitted, was to ensure Allied military supplies for his army. 'Monnet was able to persuade me that I must stress my democratic tendencies and gloss over my convictions,' Giraud later wrote. The speech also gave recognition to the French Resistance which de Gaulle was organizing in London.

◆ Like the Allies, Monnet was anxious to prevent any future dictatorship by either Giraud or de Gaulle. But meanwhile during the ensuing months, he steadily worked to equip the French army, empty the internment camps and generally liberalize the North

African regime. He also worked to help Giraud respond to the increasingly blunt moves by de Gaulle to take over the leadership of all French forces.

◆ In May, he prepared a draft for Giraud's reply to de Gaulle's telegram which set conditions for an Algiers meeting of the generals. Its main points were that they should meet in Algiers; that all questions of persons, tanks and organization should be discussed between them and that there should be an executive committee with collective responsibility and limited powers which would not be the Government of France.

◆ What Monnet proposed was to establish a basic framework for collective and therefore democratic action. Once established it would acquire its own momentum, and there would be no going back. As a French historian remarked, this was Monnet's philosophy in a nutshell.

◆ After de Gaulle arrived in Algiers, he had a three-hour talk with Monnet. His mood, Monnet reported, seemed to alternate from comparative calm to great excitability. He was very critical of the Americans and, to a lesser degree, of the British. Anglo-Saxon domination of Europe was a growing threat. If it continued after the war, France would have to lean toward Germany and Russia.

◆ In early June, de Gaulle and Giraud exchanged barbed words but later agreed to establish the French Committee of National Liberation with both as co-presidents. The committee described itself as 'the central French authority […] throughout the world.' Monnet was still positioned between the two generals in their quest to dominate the other. Despite a convivial lunch given by Churchill, with the two generals seated on either side of him, Monnet looked on with both anxiety and hope.

◆ American dismay with developments soon came with decisions of the new French Committee to enlarge itself to 14 members. De Gaulle gradually dominated the group which included

Monnet in charge of armaments and supplies. Yet Monnet was anxious to set up around both generals a collective democratic organization.

♦ When tensions arose between Eisenhower, the Allied supreme commander, and de Gaulle over military control of French forces, Monnet's turn came to make his last direct contribution of uniting the rival French factions. This time he had to satisfy not only the two generals but also Eisenhower. Monnet's press conference announced a compromise he had engineered. He knew, however, his solution [of joint control] was only temporary but it averted a complete collapse of French unity and reinforced the primacy of civil over military power.

♦ By September, thanks to Monnet's efforts, French troops had received 455,000 tons of supplies. The next month he left Algiers. His mission was to prepare supplies for France when liberated. As de Gaulle more graphically put it, Monnet was back in Washington 'to play on a broad keyboard of solutions and contacts.'

♦ Monnet ended the mission by accepting de Gaulle's offer of a role in the now-united French Resistance. He returned to Washington and spent the next two years bringing France more fully into preparation for the final push to end the war in Europe and to prepare its post-war role.

♦ Monnet was now an official representative [in Washington] of the virtual provisional Government of France. His role in bringing it to birth was important and at some points, crucial. He had not, as some (including Giraud) suspected, betrayed them by transferring his allegiance to de Gaulle. Harold Macmillan, the British representative in North Africa, wrote

France owes much to Jean Monnet. His work in Algiers was absolutely vital to any solution. He was the lubricant, even the catalyst, between two bitterly opposing factions [...] But he was an equally good friend to the British and American governments and peoples. He never swerved from his concept of close cooperation [...] during and after the war between the New World and the Old [...].

Monnet returned to Washington in late 1943. During 1944 and 1945, he worked to increase the flow of Lend-Lease supplies for France. He wrestled with the odd question of what currency to use in liberated France. He worked especially hard after the war in Europe ended to maintain and enlarge the American commitment to return France to an active role in rebuilding itself. He negotiated a large U.S. loan for this purpose in early 1946 (just after accepting de Gaulle's offer for the central role in planning France's post-war economy.)

◆ In 1945, the question was how to rebuild France. There the outward signs of penury were shabby, unpainted buildings, bare shops, poorly-clad people clumping along in wooden-soled shoes; trains with boards for windows; vélo-taxis still on the streets, and the rare buses and lorries so crowded that passengers clung on the outside.

◆ For Monnet, all this made a sad contrast with the United States but what also struck him was a basic difference in psychology. He brooded on it when he returned to Washington from a brief Paris visit and it struck him again when in April 1945, as an assistant-delegate to the [United Nations] San Francisco conference, he saw Frenchmen and other Europeans in conclave with Americans. His compatriots in particular seemed more complex, more overtly intellectual; but if they were dignified, even proud, they were also profoundly conservative – a form of timidity that hardly suited their or de Gaulle's assertions of grandeur.

◆ Four months later, this gave Monnet an opportunity. At a Washington airport, he had a brief but trenchant meeting with de Gaulle, As Monnet recalled the meeting:

> You talk about greatness, but the French are small. There will only be *grandeur* when the French are of the stature that justifies *grandeur*. They must be brought into harmony with the

rest of the world. And for that you must have more production, more productivity, if we are to transform the country... Then the French will be great, because that is their nature.

And de Gaulle said, "Yes, but would you take on the job?"

I said, "I don't know what I'll do, but I'll try."

VII. Planner

Monnet's acceptance of the job offer by Charles de Gaulle to rebuild the French economy represented a major turn in his life. Until now he had been a salesman, an advisor, a committee member, a grey eminence. Now he was to become responsible, in political terms, for reconstructing the economy of a major European power. If he ever had any doubt about his ability to undertake such a task, it is not recorded.

While still living in Washington and managing French post-war supplies from America, Monnet twice travelled back to France. He slowly assembled a small team of advisors, including Americans George Ball and Robert Nathan, both from his wartime work, and others recommended to him. He brought with him a full life of experience. He was now nearly 60 years old and not lacking in self-confidence. But how to start? Mayne describes his approach to the 'Monnet Method'.

Start with a problem. Examine it thoroughly, discuss it, go over it again and again. Find the essential element. Then an idea will emerge, usually simple. Test it with more reflection and argument. Complications will arise but stick to the point. In the end, the idea will still be simple but stronger, more direct and inevitable for having been worked on it for so long.

When the opportunity comes, act decisively. You may fail; but unless you try, you will never be sure that you might not have succeeded. Keep your final goal in mind but concentrate on what has to be done now. Progress will be gradual, practical and difficult; but if you have made the right choice, there is nothing more important than what you are doing. Once the goal is attained, it will look different; because of your action, conditions will have changed. But the fundamental point will still be the same.

Monnet admired explorers like Thor Heyerdahl whose photo he kept on his desk. Speaking of the mariners, Monnet said 'Those people chose their course, then they set out. They knew they could not turn back. Whatever the difficulties, they had only one option – to go on.'

In Algiers, Monnet had been deeply involved in French politics as a member of the French Committee of National Liberation. He was for the first time in his life virtually a minister. He soon gave up the title. But he had been wondering about a possible political career. He told an interviewer many years later,

> I hesitated then whether I should go into politics or not, because I felt that politics was the only way… of achieving the end which I thought was necessary. But after thinking it over and discussing it with my wife, I came to the conclusion: No. To go into politics ties you necessarily to a certain presentation of things… And also there is a great competition [for] who will get the power – who will be the first?… [T]he question to settle [a problem] disappears.

So in Fall 1945, Jean Monnet turned from Washington to France. He was still busy with Lend-Lease business and with negotiating the first American loan; but he now spent many hours discussing his [planning] project with a number of like-minded economists. Several of them he knew already. Robert Marjolin, tall, incisive and very youthful at 33, with bright eyes, a springy step, and a quick, winning smile, had worked with Monnet in London and Washington; he was a friend and political colleague of the veteran Socialist Leon Blum.

The engineer, Etienne Hirsch, although some years younger than Monnet, looked oddly like him with the same build and height, the same economical gestures, the same freckled skin and ready geniality. A third former colleague was Alfred Sauvy, a distinguished academic economist who introduced Monnet to Jean Fourastié, Jean Vergeot and several others who were to work on the Plan. Others in these early talks were Pierre Uri, full of ideas and humour; Paul Delouvrier, the tough, lively son of a banker with the physique of a fullback and challenging freshness of speech;

Bernard Clappier, with hooded, saturnine eyes and slicked black hair; and the enterprising Felix Gaillard, later to be one of the youngest prime ministers of France.

The task of the Plan was to inject new life and spirit into a stagnant economy made worse by war; it had to fight against what Monnet once called 'that great force which is habit.' In its founding decree, it was:

- to increase production and trade with the rest of the world;
- to raise productivity;
- to ensure full employment;
- to raise the standard of living and improve the conditions of living.

Monnet had always preferred to work with small teams. For the Paris headquarters of the Plan, he found a modest building on the left bank, on the rue de Martignac, a small island of calm in a busy city. The total staff was some twenty-five, most seconded from various ministries.

Formally, the team was organized in four divisions: technology, economics and statistics, finance and administration. In practice, Monnet's own methods were what they had always been. His desk was a trestle table, covered with papers. Close at hand were notepad and pencil. Members of the team would assemble with Monnet for discussions which seemed endless. He would listen, sometimes asking questions, sometimes heading the debate into a new direction but letting his experts run on.

Then, 'We've talked enough; we lose the thread. Do a note on it.' The note written, Monnet would read it impatiently. 'What's all this? No, no, no, no, that's not it. It was much more simple. You're too complicated. Make it more direct.' The repeated revising would begin. The final result was seldom more than two pages. It seemed so obvious that no one could disagree with what it said.

As *commissaire général*, his official mandate was an 'overall plan' but he approached it, typically, in his own way. He told an interviewer years later: 'Where do you begin?'

The economy is moved by certain factors – electricity, railroads, coal, steel... if you develop them, you develop the whole economy. Monnet asked his assistants to list these basic points, they came up with 35 key industries. This was too complicated. He reduced the list to six: coal, steel, electricity, cement, transport, and agriculture.

At the first meeting of the Plan's council in March 1946, it passed resolutions giving its modernization commissions enormous production targets for 1950: Most proved over-ambitious but a start had been made. Two days later Monnet left for Washington to back up finance minister Léon Blum in negotiating a second American loan. Their position was greatly strengthened by the Plan's existence which demonstrated both France's determination to set her house in order and her need for help from outside.

In November 1946, some five months behind schedule, Monnet was able to present the Plan itself. His report was eloquent and well written. 'Universally minded as they are by nature, the French people cannot live contentedly in a modern world unless they live (and work) in a modern way. Modernization is not a state of affairs but a state of mind.'

To produce on that scale, the report prescribed, Frenchmen would have to work an extra 8 hours a week overtime. The investment needed was nearly a quarter of the national income. At the November council meeting, Prime Minister Georges Bidault declared: 'We don't have to choose between comfort and investment; we shall only have the comfort if we have the investment.' The phrase here bore the stamp of Monnet's thinking. One after another, representatives of the trade unions, including both Christian and Communist-led, the employers' group, small businessmen and farm workers all gave their approval of the Plan.

The 'Monnet Plan,' as it came to be called, was not mandatory but indicative. 'It is an objective,' he said later. Like most objectives, it had to be adjusted as time went on. 'Jean Monnet,' as one French economist wrote, was 'among the few [...] to have the intuition' that France needed huge basic investments to get her on the new road of economic growth. 'It was a truth not well received in business circles,' he added. Monnet's achievement, as in Washington during the war, was to get them to raise their sights.

There was one problem, however, that Monnet's Plan, and France itself, could not solve alone – the country's inability to pay its way in the world. Nor would France be alone in her post-war plight. Outside help could only come from the United States.

An indication of this problem came in February 1947 when Britain stopped aid to Greece and Turkey. [In its place] the Truman Doctrine the next month pledged the United States 'to support free peoples which are resisting attempted subjugation by armed minorities or by outside pressure.'

It also prompted action by Dean Acheson, a friend of Monnet for many years. In November 1943 they had spent three weeks together in the unlikely setting of Atlantic City [New Jersey, at an international aid conference]. 'Happily in those weeks,' wrote Acheson, 'we had long walks on the famous boardwalk along the winter ocean' where Monnet argued about 'Europe's need to escape its historic parochialism.'

Now it was Acheson who set in motion a fresh study of U.S. foreign aid. He told an audience in May 1947 that

> European recovery cannot be complete until the various parts of Europe's economy are working together in a harmonious whole. The achievement of a coordinated European economy remains a fundamental objective of our foreign policy.

The next month, at Harvard University, Secretary of State George Marshall echoed these ideas when he launched the plan that bears his name.

As head of the Plan and as an old acquaintance of Prime Minister Georges Bidault, Jean Monnet was doubly involved in the French response to the Marshall Plan. He produced for Bidault several important briefs. An historian of the Marshall Plan said Monnet 'made an enormous contribution not only formally but also in resolving matters behind the scenes.'

He was able to do this because he was on such good terms with the Americans. In Paris he was a close friend of David Bruce, now U.S. ambassador. Another faithful ally was a young U.S. Treasury Department official at the embassy, William Tomlinson. In Spring 1948, Monnet was back in Washington, formally negotiating for wheat but also arguing endlessly about Europe's broader future.

When the time came to prepare European machinery for dealing with Marshall Plan aid, Monnet seconded his assistant, Robert Marjolin, to work in the French delegation. The British and several other governments were at first reluctant to establish any permanent European institution *[to manage aid]* but at length, after strong pressure from the Americans, urged on by Monnet, it was agreed to establish the Organization for European Economic Cooperation (OEEC). Marjolin was named its first secretary-general and, on Monnet's suggestion, he was given ex officio right to initiate proposals, a precedent used later in the institutions of the European Community.

The Marshall Plan and OEEC completed a foundation for Western Europe's post-war recovery. Between 1948 and 1952, Europe received Marshall aid totalling $13.15 billion of which the $3.1 billion went to the United Kingdom and $2.7 billion to France. It thereby initiated economic cooperation and removed most quantitative restrictions from European trade. The existence of such a permanent body [OEEC] prepared the way for the European Community.

Nevertheless, the organization disappointed Monnet's and many Americans' initial hopes. It involved no real delegation of sovereignty; a number of its member states deliberately kept it weak.

Even the idea of a 'master plan' for Europe, long urged by Monnet and U.S. officials, finally had to be abandoned. Several plans for customs unions appeared but none survived except for one made in 1944 by Belgium, Luxembourg and the Netherlands (Benelux).

Military cooperation had a different outcome. In June 1948, a Soviet blockade of Berlin was answered by the Berlin airlift which was by December carrying 4,500 tons a day to the city. Earlier, the U.S. began talks with Canada and European powers that would lead to the negotiations of the North Atlantic Treaty [NATO].

But in economic cooperation there were outstanding barriers. Most hesitant of all was Great Britain, still at that time convinced that she had not in a true sense lost the war. In the end, the initiative for unity in Europe, as distinct from cooperation, came from France to find a first partner in the enterprise, she had to look across the Rhine instead of across the Channel.

Monnet had made a final attempt in 1949 to bring Britain and France into closer economic cooperation with a hopeful political component. He invited Sir Edwin Plowden to his country home in Houjarray, outside Paris. Plowden was head of planning for the U.K. Treasury. Although some years Monnet's junior, he resembled him both in temperament and in the variety of his experience; it was natural that quick mutual sympathy arose between them.

Monnet's country home was an I-shaped farmhouse, with a low, flagged drawing room full of Madame Monnet's paintings and family keepsakes; its tall, rather rickety French windows look across the gardens and fields – a view combining the gentleness of the English countryside with the stricter charm of the French.

After extensive preliminaries, the time came for them to ask a crucial question: What happened if France and Britain were to draw up a joint plan? Could they, in effect, pool their resources? Could they lead the way?

Now a basic misunderstanding began to steal over the discussion. Monnet may have been at fault for not explaining clearly enough what he was proposing. Plowden may have found the idea too radical to believe. They began to talk at cross purposes. Plowden suggested that two main subjects required study: Britain was short of food; France was short of coal. Could they not help meet each other's needs? 'Could not the respective burdens on their agricultural sectors be reduced or ended?'

The Houjarray meeting had been very friendly; Plowden became one of Monnet's trusted English friends. They exchanged in the coming weeks much information. But there was no repetition of the meeting at Houjarray. So Monnet's second attempt at some form of Franco-British union failed. The first, in 1940, was rejected by a French government in extremis; the second was ignored by a British government intent on other things.

Had there been a joint plan, or even an economic union, the whole future of post-war Europe and of Britain's uneasy role in it would have been different. But a different Europe would have presupposed a different Britain – ready to make a decisive choice, then settle the details. It was a pattern that was to be repeated with even more obviously fateful results in the following years.

VIII. European

'We're in difficulties. That's a good sign.
If we weren't, we'd never change anything.
And making Europe means changing things.'

'Mr Europe' is the rather hackneyed nickname given to Jean Monnet by the American press. He accepts it with a slight grimace. He has also been called 'the father of Europe.' 'H'm... don't you mean grandfather?' he once answered. 'And besides there are many fathers of Europe. It's a collective effort – action in common.' But he seemed pleased.

Even so, in calling Monnet a 'European', it would be wrong to think of him as merely a European patriot. The greater part of his life has been spent elsewhere. In March 1948, talking with an acquaintance from the French foreign office, he said: 'I have never lived so much in my own country as in the last two years, and I'm beginning to understand Her'. He spoke sometimes of the qualities of Europeans – the energies and ideas they have contributed to civilization, their moderation, their variety, their concern for individuals and for what would now be called 'the quality of life.'

But he differed fundamentally from those European militants for whom Europe seemed to be associated with nostalgia, with old-fashioned Catholicism, with "Mediterranean values" with faint anti-Americanism, or with the classical Greco-Roman past. There was nothing 'Carolingian' about Monnet's view of the European Community: he has always seen it as the germ of a better and less nationalistic form of relations between states. In his view, as he put it in the preface of a book of mine *[which Mayne himself may have helped write]*,

The Common Market is not a static creation: it is a new and dynamic phase in the development of our civilization. The essential characteristic of this new phase is that nations have now begun to accept that their problems are joint problems and cannot be settled by national measures alone.

The virtue of the Common Market is to use this realization creatively, by applying joint measures through common rules and institutions – the method which, in other spheres is already acknowledged as the basis of civilized society [...].

One day, perhaps, the new method adopted in the Common Market may be used to meet even broader challenges and to create even greater opportunities.

For Monnet, in other words, Europe is partially 'a building block' for gradually organizing a more stable, just and peaceful world.

Some saw this as a visionary aspiration: but it grew quite naturally and gradually from Monnet's practical experiences. Ever since World War I, he had seen the need for nations to recognize how many of their problems they shared with each other, and could only solve collectively through common rules and common institutions. Their first collective effort, the League of Nations, had notably failed. Its successor, the United Nations, looked scarcely more promising. Undeterred, Monnet returned to the attack in the later years of World War II.

The Beginnings

In Algiers, in a note written in August 1943, Monnet began to set down his ideas about the future of Europe. His starting point was the series of mistakes that had been made after World War I:

> There will be no peace [he wrote] if States are reconstituted on a basis of National Sovereignty with all that this implies [...] If the countries of Europe again protect themselves against each other, it will be again necessary to build

vast armies. Some countries [...] will be able to do so; to others this will be forbidden [...] Europe will once more be founded on fear.

The countries of Europe are too small to guarantee their peoples the prosperity that modern conditions make possible and therefore necessary. They need larger markets. They must also avoid using [...] their resources to maintain so-called 'key' industries for national defence [...] Their prosperity, and the social developments that are indispensable, can only be ensured if the States of Europe form a federation [...] which makes them a single economic unit.

Monnet continued to ponder and discuss these ideas throughout the rest of World War II. Nearly a year later, in July 1944, just back from Washington, he had a long talk with Harold Macmillan.

In Monnet's view, [Macmillan noted] the whole future of Europe depended upon the solution of the German problem and the effective reduction [...] of the German war potential. A full United States of Europe is still beyond realization but he felt that a strong League, possibly combined with interstate trade and monetary arrangements, could be made effective [...].

In this England must take the lead and France must support her. The smaller States – Belgium, Holland, Denmark, the Scandinavian powers, Spain, Italy – must be both contributors to and beneficiaries of this Western system.

In the United States, Monnet expounded similar ideas to the journalist John Davenport, who reported them in the August 1944 *Fortune* magazine. Monnet was convinced, he said, that the United Nations, like the League, would

be only a 'switchboard' through which nations can communicate with each other. It will involve no real giving up of sovereignty. This is not going to happen on a world scale

[…] and let us not blind ourselves this time by the picture of impressive machinery; to be really tough, things need to be done […] for peace.

Davenport continued:

What are those tough things? For Monnet, as for most Europeans, the toughest questions of all are Germany and European unity. Monnet would like to see Germany shocked and stripped of part of her industrial potential, with possibly the great Ruhr coal and iron fields run by a European authority for the benefit of all nations, including a demilitarized Germany.

But this in turn implies a Europe far more unified than before the war. Here he would like to see […] a true yielding of sovereignty by European nations to some kind of central union […]. But where to begin? And how far to go? And could England be brought in? For without England, Monnet sees, the concept of a unified Europe turns all too quickly into a Germanized Europe all over again.

In the midst of total war, it was a natural enough worry. And the remedy, in Monnet's eyes, was a 'Europeanized Germany' safely linked with its partners […]

***

Monnet's ideas on this subject, as on others, were far from new. Ever since Pierre Dubois in the early 14th century had proposed a European council of 'wise, expert and faithful men,' writers and theorists had been pressing various forms of European unity. Their motives had been as diverse as their proposals. Some, like Dubois himself, or Antoine Marigny, Richard Hooker, the duc de Sully, or Leibniz, wanted to restore the supposed unity of mediaeval Christendom. Some, like Dubois again, or Emeric Gruce, Grotius, William Penn, the Abbe de Saint Pierre, Jeremy Bentham, Kant or Victor Considerant, saw a united Europe as the key to 'a perpetual peace.'

Monnet had scarcely heard of, let alone read, a number of these prophets; but he and they had one thing in common: the aim was a new international order... centered on Europe which was then the focus of the civilized world.

Paradoxically, however, Europe's growing awareness of other continents was to be one ingredient in the so-called 'European idea.' The contrast between Europe and the other parts of the world led some to espouse a form of European patriotism, or even chauvinism, while others, perhaps less parochial, were inspired by the example of the American United States.

George Washington, in a letter to Lafayette, was one of the first to predict that there would one day be 'United States of Europe:' and the phrase was used later, not always approvingly, by the Italian statesman Francesco Grinni, by Victor Hugo, by Proudhon, and by Lenin and Trotsky. 'In a capitalistic regime,' wrote Lenin, 'the United States of Europe would be either impossible or reactionary.' But Trotsky, not for the first time, disagreed with him. In a moment of remarkable foresight, he wrote: 'Not only the question of the Ruhr, that is of European fuel and metal, but also the question of repartition, may perfectly well be settled in the framework of the United States of Europe.'

World wars, spreading from European quarrels, gave fresh thrust to similar ideas. In 1933 Monnet's friend and colleague, Arthur Salter, published a paper "The United States of Europe":

Zollvereins [customs unions] [he wrote] have often been preached, not infrequently attempted, but never, I think, realized except under conditions of an overwhelming political motive and an extremely close political association between the countries concerned [...]. The commercial and tariff policy of European states is so central and crucial a part of their general policy [...] that a common political authority [...] would be for every country almost as important as [...] the national governments and

would in effect reduce the latter to the status of munici-
pal authorities [...] the United States of Europe must be a
political reality or it cannot be an economic one.

After the holocaust of World War I, indeed, one statesman, Aristide Briand, took up the idea, only to have it buried in a series
of meetings held by a study committee of the League of Nations,
most of whose members were both sceptical and condescending.

Only during and after World War II did the notion of a united
Europe become potentially a matter of practical politics. Refugees
like Don Luigi Sturzo and Count Coudenhove-Kalergi; resistance
fighters like Altiero Spinelli, Alfred Mozer and Hendrik Brugmans, writers like Albert Camus and George Orwell – all helped
to keep the idea alive; but now the statesmen were with them. In
October 1942, Winston Churchill had already put the idea of a
'United States of Europe' to the War Cabinet and in March 1943
broadcast an appeal for a post-war 'Council of Europe.'

General de Gaulle imagined 'a strategic and economic federation
between France, Belgium, Luxembourg and the Netherlands to
which Great Britain might adhere.' Pope Pius XII even suggested
'a close union of the European states inspired by Catholicism.'
Then, in July 1944 resistance leaders of many creeds and political
persuasions met to affirm that 'Federal union alone could ensure
the preservation of liberty and civilization on the continent of
Europe, bring about economic recovery and enable the German
people to play a peaceful role in European affairs.'

But it was Churchill again, speaking at Zurich University in September 1946 who expressed most eloquently what many others
were feeling:

> If Europe were once united in the sharing of the common
> inheritance, there would be no limit to the happiness, to
> the prosperity and glory which its three or four hundred
> million people would enjoy [...]. What is this sovereign
> remedy? It is to recreate the European Family or as such

of it as we can and provide it with a structure under which it can dwell in peace, in safely and in freedom. We must build a kind of United States of Europe [...].

Right wing or left wing, clerical or anti-clerical, liberal or directed, 'Atlantic' or 'third force' – all these views believed that a united Europe was the precondition for achieving their other aims. In December 1947 the leaders among them set up an International Committee of the Movements for European Unity which organized the Council of Europe in The Hague in 1948. More than 750 European statesmen attended [...] At the end of its proceedings, it called for political and economic union in Europe, a European Assembly and a European Court of Human Rights.

Eventually, after very energetic lobbying, the governments of the five Brussels Pact powers – Britain, France and the three Benelux countries – were persuaded to set up a study committee which came forward with less far reaching proposals. Further disagreements followed but finally in May 1949, the Brussels Pact powers and five other countries initialled the Statute of the Council of Europe.

The Council of Europe was the first European organization to be explicitly political. Its headquarters was established, symbolically, in Strasbourg on the Franco-German frontier although Germany did not join until 1951. Its Convention for the Protection of Human Rights, backed by a Human Rights Commission and a court, are permanent monuments to its founders' aims.

Behind their apparent unanimity, there were serious disputes. Even Churchill's Zurich speech had implied that Great Britain would not form part of the 'United States of Europe'; and it was largely under British pressure that the Council's assembly never acquired the legislative status its original sponsors had envisaged. At the end of the first session, its President Paul-Henri Spaak declared: 'I came to Strasbourg convinced of the need for a United

States of Europe. I leave with the certainty that union is possible.' Yet two years later he resigned in protest against inaction from the Committee of Ministers.

Twenty year later, looking back on his own days in the Committee, Spaak wrote 'Of all the international bodies I have known, I have never found any more timorous or more impotent.'

Later, the Organization for European Economic Cooperation, with no overtly political mandate, probably did as much as the Council of Europe to increase the sense of solidarity among its members and thereby prepare the further steps toward unity that were soon to come.

***

Jean Monnet was not present at The Hague Congress of May 1948. Part of that Spring he spent in Washington, negotiating for wheat on behalf of the French government. After so long away from the United States, he was impressed again by its strength and energy – 'a dynamic force,' he told French Prime Minister Robert Schuman 'which springs from the very nature of each individual.' Combined with America's vast resources, this tended to make the United States the leader in any relationship with European countries; but Europe would one day have to stand on its own feet. To do so, it would have to make a joint effort in which Germany's contribution, which was indispensable, could safely be merged.

When Monnet arrived in Washington at the end of March 1948, the 'Cold War' had reached a climax. One by one, the countries of Eastern Europe had seen coalition governments ousted by Communist pressure, threats, fraud and even violence. One by one, they had been absorbed into the Soviet empire. Meanwhile, in Western Europe, Britain, France and the Benelux countries had signed the Brussels Pact on defence matters, a forerunner to NATO. On March 20, with Monnet still in Washington, the Soviet delegation walked out of the four-power control council in Berlin.

In America, the mood was grim and fatalistic. War seemed likely, if not inevitable and if it came, Western Europe would be the first victim.

But this state of mind was temporary. In April, Monnet, still in Washington, wrote to both Schuman and Georges Bidault, the French Foreign Minister. To Bidault he said

> During the past three weeks, I have witnessed what I believe is an important transformation of the American point of view on [...] Russia and war. When I arrived, the dominant idea was preparation for war – there was general acceptance of the inevitable result, the occupation of Europe by Russia. Now thought is devoted above all to means of preventing war. The idea is even emerging that *Détente* will perhaps be possible.

The seeds of the Atlantic alliance, in fact, were already being sown. But as Monnet told Schuman

> We must realize [...] that America is animated essentially by a will to action at home and abroad. I cannot but be struck by the nature of the relations which risk being established between this great country and the countries of Europe if they remain in their present form and mentality. In my opinion, Europe cannot remain 'dependent' [...] without harmful results both here and in Europe.

To Bidault, Monnet added these words about the impact of Marshall Plan aid:

> In a large measure we are going to be dependent on this country, both for our economic life and for our national security. This situation cannot be maintained for long without great danger. Today we are the stake in the game. We must rapidly transform this situation into one of independence and collaboration. America is neither

reactionary nor imperialist. Her contribution is not given in order to control us. It will stop if there is no sign of effort on our part [...].

Monnet does not mention, in his pleas from Washington, the pronounced (if narrowly-based) congressional sentiment in 1947-48 that the Europeans must unite to avoid another devastating world war. Perhaps he was not aware, in his exclusive dealings with the executive branch, of these congressional voices which said clearly that European unity was the price for continued American support, both military and economic. But it was a message in tune with Monnet's.

Monnet then made reference to the sixteen nations which earlier had signed the Paris Convention setting up the Organization for European Economic Cooperation. But what... was Monnet now proposing [to Bidault]?

> I believe that only the creation of a Federation of the West, including England, will enable us to solve our problems quickly enough and finally to prevent war. I am aware of all the difficulties, but I see no other solution [...].

To Schuman, Monnet put the point with no less force:

> All of my reflections and observations lead me to a conclusion which for me is now a profound conviction. To meet the present situation, to face the dangers that threaten us, and to match the American effort, the countries of Western Europe must turn their own efforts into a truly European effort. This will be possible only through a Federation of the West.

In isolation, this phrase might seem to imply an 'Atlantic' federation including the United States. But, rather, as the context of Churchill's words in Zurich had made it clear that his 'United States of Europe' was to be confined to the Continent, so the context of Monnet's remarks here revealed that he was speaking of Western Europe, not the future Western alliance.

The Schuman Plan

Monnet's proposals had no immediate effect. For the rest of 1948 and until the following Spring, attention focused instead on the Soviet land blockage of Berlin and on the astonishing airlift that flew food, consumer goods, fuel and even raw materials into the city for more than eleven months. Against this background the North Atlantic Treaty Organization (NATO) and the Council of Europe were formed that year.

The NATO alliance ensured Europe security and the Council of Europe inspired many hopes: but neither fulfilled the need that Monnet had pointed out. The alliance linked the United States and its Canadian neighbour with ten separate European countries – one giant and eleven comparative dwarfs. The Council of Europe, for all its founders' intentions, did little to unite Europeans in an entity comparable with the United States.

'I was impatient,' said Monnet later, 'with all these generalities leading nowhere. All that we'd known at that time, the Council of Europe and all the organizations like the League of Nation, were on the basis of complete national sovereignty. They were based on the notion of everyone explaining his position, but there was no formula, no mechanism or no institution, to reach a decision. Explaining, yes; decisions, no.'

As usual, the problem for Monnet was: where to begin. In April 1949, he made a first attempt, proposing joint planning and ultimately economic union between Britain and France. Then, as in 1940 – although for very different reasons, he had failed. But there was still urgent need for action. The problem of Germany, in particular, was becoming acute by the autumn of 1949, there were two German states – and the Soviet Union had acknowledged that it possessed the atomic bomb. The 'Cold War' had become the 'balance of terror,' with a restless, divided Germany dangerously straddling the two sides.

The prospect of German reunification now seemed remote but for the Western Allies the German Federal Republic by itself posed a problem. Konrad Adenauer, elected chancellor in Sept 1949, had startled a press conference by announcing that the Federal Republic hoped to join not only the Council of Europe but also NATO.

Under the three-power statute, which came into force the same month, a number of key questions including armaments, reparations, decartelization and foreign policy were reserved to the Allied high commissioners who had taken the place of military authorities; but it was becoming clear that this system of tutelage could not be permanent.

Inevitably, at least Western Germany would once more become an active participant in international affairs. But on this subject the Allies were deeply divided; their differences centred round the fate of German heavy industry. During the war and immediately after, some had been determined to keep post-war Germany in permanent economic subjugation. Having suffered from the excesses of German nationalism, they believed that the only way to tame it was by force.

In this respect, Henry Morgenthau's notorious proposal for 'pastoralizing' Germany was fundamentally similar to the demands and policies of the Soviet Union. Both America and Britain, after briefly flirting with the Morgenthau plan, rejected it. In Churchill's words, 'England would be chained to a dead body.'

The question had therefore begun to be less that of whether to allow the Ruhr to be rehabilitated than how this could be done in safety. Ernest Bevin, the British foreign secretary, was only one of many to suggest international control; this took the shape of the International Ruhr Authority set up in 1948. During the negotiations which led up to it, the United States insisted chiefly on rebuilding the Ruhr and France on the need to control it. The British position was somewhere in between.

It was scarcely surprising that when the Ruhr authority came to take practical decisions, some found it too stringent, and others too lax; It soon became clear that its days were numbered. In attenuated form, it was a further attempt to deal with Germany as a passive object of Allied policy. As such, it was increasingly incompatible with the Federal Republic's changing legal, political, economic and human situation. To Jean Monnet, especially, continued unilateral control seemed both unjust and unwise.

'There was still in many people's minds,' he recalled afterwards, 'the notion that the peace with Germany should be based on the notion of superiority – domination – which was the peace of 1918. I felt that there would be a catastrophe.'

Monnet had long been convinced that equality was the only basis on which nations, like men, could come to terms with each other. This applied, he believed, with especial force in the case of Germany. Any permanent effort to suppress the national feelings of the German people would in the end only exacerbate them more. Already, at the League of Nations, Monnet had quarrelled with the *revanchiste* notions of Raymond Poincaré. Then *revanche* [revenge] had helped lead to Hitler. A similar danger seemed far more remote now but decisions on Germany's future were pending which might have equally profound and far reaching effects.

Between France and Germany relations were uneasy not only over the Ruhr but also over the Saar whose national status *[between the two countries]* remained in dispute. Meanwhile, the United States continued to press for a more active contribution by Germany to Western Europe's economy – if not, as yet, to its defence. A fresh meeting of British, French and US foreign ministers was scheduled for Spring 1950 after a failed attempt the previous Autumn to find agreement. What its outcome might be no one cared to predict; but in Paris there was deep uneasiness about what lay ahead.

The Autumn meeting had a significant consequence. There Dean Acheson and Ernest Bevin had pressed Robert Schuman to come up with a solution to the 'German problem' at their next meeting. The

French foreign minister took the challenge but without knowing how he would respond. According to his chief aide, Bernard Clappier, the challenge was met the following April when Monnet presented an idea which happily, matched Schuman's need. Details are in FRUS 1949 III 579-603 and 621-625; in Clappier's OH in FJME; and in JMM 299-304.

In this situation, Monnet saw both danger and opportunity. The danger, fundamentally, was a threat to peace. The opportunity was to sublimate the German question somehow in the beginning of a united Europe.

✱✱✱

This idea was far from new. Winston Churchill had already proposed it in his Zurich speech in September 1946:

> I am now going to say something that will astonish you. The first step in the re-creation of the European family must be a partnership between France and Germany. In this way only can France recover the moral leadership of Europe. There can be no revival of Europe without a spiritually great France and a spiritually great Germany.

'Time may be short…' Churchill had added: but his words led to nothing beyond the Council of Europe of which Germany was not yet a member. More recently, Konrad Adenauer had made specific proposals, reverting to an idea he had championed in the 1920s: that 'a lasting peace between France and Germany can only be attained through the establishment of a community of economic interests between the two countries.'

On New Year's Day 1949, the minister-president of North Rhine-Westphalia had suggested a plan to which 'Germany would bring the Ruhr, France the ore resources of Lorraine, both of them the Saar, and Belgium and Luxembourg their heavy industries.' Adenauer had revived this project in January 1950 in a conversation with John McCloy, the US High Commissioner. Then in March he proposed a political union between Germany and France to be open also to Britain, Italy and the Benelux countries.

Charles de Gaulle, then in opposition and head of his political party, had hailed Adenauer's idea but no European government had seriously taken it on. The French government, now headed by Georges Bidault with Robert Schuman as his foreign minister – a neat reversal of roles – had simply declared its willingness to listen to any 'concrete proposals.'

Monnet had been very impressed by Adenauer's proposals and had discussed them with many people. "Have you seen that?' he asked one chance visitor to his rue de Martignac office, showing him the newspaper reports. The visitor was Paul Reuter, law professor at Aix and a legal adviser to the French foreign office. What did he think of Adenauer's idea for a common Parliament? It would have to have something to do, said Reuter; otherwise it would be no more effective than the Council of Europe. Monnet agreed.

But what about establishing a new political entity to deal with Europe's 'industrial triangle' – Holland, Belgium, Luxembourg, the Ruhr, the Saar and Lorraine? Impossible, Reuter answered: they would never accept a common political authority, nor would France and Germany agree to such a thing. Perhaps an economic grouping – or, better, a joint plan for the region, spanning the frontiers? 'Come back tomorrow morning,' said Monnet. 'We must go on with this.'

Next day, Reuter returned to continue the discussion, joined by Etienne Hirsch and Pierre Uri, Monnet's assistants on the French Plan. Their debate went on all day and was resumed on Sunday at Houjarray, Monnet's country home. Gradually it took a new turn.

What they had been proposing, Uri argued, was a combine for heavy industry with a number of nationalized firms centrally controlled. That would never work; the Germans would fight it and the Americans would mistrust it. Why not instead form a single market for coal and steel – not confined merely to the 'industrial triangle" but extending over Western Europe as a whole?

It was only later that this acquired the names 'Community' and 'Common Market' but already some familiar outlines were emerging. That Sunday evening, Monnet asked Reuter to produce a short note on the subject. He brought it to the office at 9 the next morning. When it was typed out, Monnet and his colleagues worked it over again. The full proposal was to go through thirty versions before reaching its final form.

But time was pressing. The foreign ministers London conference was only a few weeks away. Monnet asked to see the prime minister to discuss the project but Bidault's timetable was full. Monnet then sent one version with a covering letter via Bidault's chief aide. The result was disappointing. Bidault was more interested in a proposal for an Atlantic high council which he made himself earlier that month; he never replied to Monnet's letter.

Fortunately, Monnet had another idea. Some weeks before he had discussed his project with Bernard Clappier, who was Foreign Minister Schuman's chief aide. Already, two years earlier, when Schuman headed the French government, Monnet had found him receptive to 'European' ideas.

A quiet, shrewd, stooping, rather bookish bachelor, he was two years older than Monnet and in some respects his opposite. Monnet was a stocky, sceptical Charentais; Schuman described himself as 'a Catholic from the Moselle'. Although born in Luxembourg he came of French stock. His father had been a landowner near Thionville (Lorraine) some miles south of Luxembourg. He had fought for France in the Franco-Prussian War and gone into voluntary exile in Luxembourg when Alsace and Lorraine was annexed by Germany in 1871.

Robert Schuman had been educated in Luxembourg and studied law at various German universities. He spoke German fluently throughout his life. He was typical, in fact, of those 'men of the frontier' who felt most keenly the tragedy of Europe's national conflicts: Joseph Bech, also from Luxembourg; Paul-Henri Spaak from divided Belgium; Alcide de Gasperi from the Italian Trentino; Konrad Adenauer from the disputed Rhineland.

World War I had convinced Schuman that Franco-German reconciliation was vital for peace and after Alsace and Lorraine were returned to post-war France, he had entered the French Assembly. Like Monnet, he had warned French politicians against victimizing Germany and he had supported Aristide Briand's interwar proposal for a united Europe. During the World War II occupation of France, Schuman had been arrested and imprisoned by the Nazis then released under police surveillance from which he had escaped to live in hiding.

After liberation, he had helped form the Christian Democrat party. As foreign minister, he had supported the policy of cautiously relaxing Allied controls on Germany. His bitter personal experiences, his religious faith, his present responsibilities and his worries for the future – all made him likely to respond to a practical proposal for reconciling France and Germany.

Monnet had therefore asked Clappier to sound out Schuman's reactions. When he did, Schuman showed great interest and Clappier arranged to see Monnet again to take the matter further. Unfortunately, when the time came, urgent business made Clappier miss the rendezvous; Monnet assumed that Schuman's interest had waned. Then Clappier sent his apologies and all was well.

On the same day as Monnet wrote to Bidault, he gave his draft to Clappier with a handwritten note for Schuman. Clappier passed it on the next day just as the minister was leaving for a weekend at his rather shabby country house near Metz. By now time was short, very short: there was less than a fortnight before the foreign ministers meeting.

According to his oral history Clappier told Monnet at their meeting of the charge given Schuman by Dean Acheson and Ernest Bevin at the September 1949 meeting in Washington to come up with a solution to the 'German Problem' at the May 1950 meeting of the three foreign ministers. This challenge weighed on the French Foreign Minister, he said.

One month later, Dean Acheson told the US European ambassadors meeting in Paris that France, not Britain, was the key to European integration. (Clappier OH, FJME; FRUS 1949, III 599-607; 621-25. and FRUS 1949 IV 469-72.)

In the peace of his study, surrounded by his fine collection of manuscripts and books, Schuman read and pondered Monnet's paper. That Sunday, April 30, he made up his mind. When he returned to Paris the next day, Clappier met him at the Gare de l'Est. 'I've read the note,' Schuman said. 'It's interesting. I'll make it my affair." Then he telephoned Monnet: 'I accept. For me, it's decided.'

Two days later on May 3 Schuman broached the matter with some of his cabinet colleagues, in purposely general terms. Only two of them, both Monnet friends, fully realized its implication: one was René Pleven, the other René Mayer. To others, Schuman seemed to be talking about some technical scheme of limited scope and interest, something to do with coal and steel.

That same day, however, Monnet and his colleagues at the rue de Martignac office put the final touches to a far more comprehensive memorandum which explained the political significance of their 'modest proposal.' Monnet sent it to both Schuman and Bidault the following day. After noting that men's minds were 'becoming focused on an object at once simple and dangerous: the cold war.' It included these passages:

> The course of events must be changed. To do this men's minds must be changed. Words are not enough. Only immediate action on an essential point can change the

present static situation [...]. The German situation is rapidly becoming a cancer that will be dangerous to peace in the near future.

After reviewing the historic roles of France and Germany, the document cites the challenge to the countries of Western Europe:

Europe has never existed. It is not the addition of sovereign nations set together in councils which makes an entity of them. We must genuinely create Europe [...].
This creation, at the moment when association with an America of such power is in question, is indispensable in order to make clear that the countries of Europe are not taking the easy way out, that they are not giving way to fear, that they believe in themselves and that they are setting up without delay the first machinery for building a Europe within the new community of free and peaceful peoples.
At the present moment, Europe can be brought to birth only by France. Only France can speak and act [...]. If she takes the initiative that will eliminate fear, revive faith in the future and make possible the creation of a force for peace, she will have liberated Europe.

Once again there was no response from Bidault. But Schuman, his mind made up, was now actively involved in the plan that was to bear his name. Shortly after returning from his weekend home, he came to lunch with Monnet and his colleagues. The day was warm. 'Make yourself comfortable, Monsieur le Président' said Monnet. 'It's stifling in here. Why not take off your jacket? I'll do the same – it's a habit I picked up in America.' At first, Schuman demurred. 'We seldom lunch in shirtsleeves at the Quai d'Orsay,' he said. 'And besides, I wear braces.' The ice was broken.

Monnet assured Schuman that as a man of obvious integrity – transparently honest as well as shrewd – he was uniquely fitted to bring off a dramatic act of statesmanship without being accused of plotting. They both agreed, however, that secrecy and surprise were essential to its success.

Throughout that week, they consulted none of the government's normal advisers or civil servants. 'We knew,' said Schuman, 'that from the beginning, and especially at the beginning, the idea would raise doubts and ever a certain hostility. Ordinary methods and widespread prior consultations would have led to countless and endless delays.' Nevertheless, 'before launching our bombshell we had to know what reaction it would get from our most important partners; Chief among them [...] was the German government and [...] before May 9 we secured agreement in principle from the Federal chancellor.'

In his memoirs, Adenauer was later to declare that there had been no prior negotiations between Paris and Bonn, and that on the morning the 'bombshell' was finally launched, he still did not know that it was due that day. Both statements are true but both were somewhat misleading. On Friday, May 5, Schuman sent a friend, a private businessman, as his personal emissary to Bonn. Schuman's messenger took the Paris-Cologne night express. Early the next morning, it stopped at Remagen where the French High Commissioner, André François-Poncet, was waiting with a car to drive the thirteen miles north along the Rhine to the capital.

In Bonn, in the chancellery office in the Palais Schaumberg, with only an interpreter as a witness, Schuman's envoy outlined the plan to Adenauer, handing him both an early draft and a personal letter from Schuman. He then withdrew, adding that he would be glad to take any message back to Paris. For more than two hours, while the messenger waited, Adenauer discussed the proposal with his foreign affairs adviser, Herbert Blankenhorn. Then he drafted an enthusiastic response. It was taken back on that evening's night express and was in Schuman's hand on Sunday morning, May 7.

That same Sunday, a second non-French statesman was let into the secret. Dean Acheson, the US secretary of state, was due in London the coming week for the foreign ministers' conference. After what he called 'a long, strenuous, wearying winter and spring,' State Department colleagues had urged him to 'get a few days rest' and please Schuman by starting early and going via Paris for some friendly talks with the French.

Acheson landed at Orly airport on Sunday morning, May 7. The US Ambassador David Bruce told him of an unusual request from the French foreign office. Instead of a courtesy call on Monday, Schuman had suggested a private meeting that very afternoon.

Schuman quickly disclosed to Acheson and Bruce what he was about to put formally before the French cabinet. 'Almost my first thought,' wrote Acheson afterwards, 'was [...] that the arrangement could become a giant cartel.' Schuman and Monnet soon reassured him.

Later, the point became clearer when, with no need for an interpreter, Acheson and Bruce talked with Monnet who brought with him John McCloy, the US high commissioner for Germany. By contrast with Bidault's plan for an Atlantic high council, thought Acheson, 'Monnet's apparently more limited and modest plan was, in reality, more imaginative and far-reaching.'

Schuman and Monnet asked Acheson 'not to speak to any of our colleagues about it, not to send cables, or to have memoranda transcribed.' President Truman was at that moment travelling in the far west to inaugurate a dam. It would have been risky to contact his train. Acheson and Bruce therefore sent a first 'eyes only' telegram to the president, saying only that 'an important development might (repeat might) take place within a few days.' In the meantime, should rumours begin to come from Europe, Acheson asked the president not to comment. 'The danger was,' he later wrote, 'that the first report of the plan would arouse fears in the departments of justice and commerce similar to my own first thoughts [...].'

Monnet and his colleagues, meanwhile, were putting the final touches to the text of their proposal. It incorporated suggestions from many quarters. Last minute changes included the removal of several provocative sentences including 'Europe must be organized on a federal basis' and 'This proposal has an essential political objective to make a breach in the ramparts of national sovereignty [...] narrow enough to secure consent but deep enough to open the way toward the unity that is essential to peace.'

In his memoirs, Monnet notes the prudent removal of these provocative sentences but makes clear that their intent was still there as obvious goals of the Schuman Plan (JMM, 296).

Finally, by the evening of May 8, the text was ready. Monnet asked to hear it read one last time. He asked everyone to stand. That night, the rue de Martignac team burned the preliminary notes and drafts. The text of the introduction was taken the next morning by Clappier to Schuman, ready for the crucial cabinet meeting.

At the office, Monnet and colleagues waited by the telephone. For an hour, there was no news. Then, at 11 am, the ministers came out of the meeting. Monnet wondered if Schuman had tried and failed. In fact, it was an adjournment and for good reason. The night before, Schuman had sent an emissary from his private office to Bonn with the final text and a handwritten letter. An urgent note went to Adenauer, in a cabinet meeting saying that Schuman needed an answer right away. Wasting no time, Adenauer gave it by telephone.

When the French cabinet resumed its meeting, Schuman was able to put forward his proposal. He read a short note, once again stressing its technical aspect and speaking rapidly. The Prime Minister, Bidault, hesitated; later he was nonplussed to find the identical proposal from Monnet at the back of a desk drawer. But Pleven and Mayer backed Schuman and the cabinet authorized him to go ahead.

Later, at 6 p.m. about a hundred journalists assembled for a press conference in the ornate and gilded Salon de l'Horloge. Schuman entered and made his way quickly to the empty place at the head of the hollow square of green-baize covered tables. Adjusting a pair of heavy framed spectacles, he began to read from the paper held in his hand. The traditional setting contrasted sharply with what he had to say.

'It is no longer the moment for vain words, but for a bold act – a constructive act.' The words were Schuman's own; that afternoon he had written a brief preamble to the basic text. But the sentiment was also Monnet's. 'France has acted, and the consequences of her action may be immense. We hope they will.'

> 'She has acted essentially in the cause of peace. For peace to have a real chance, there must first be a Europe. Five years almost to the day after Germany's unconditional surrender, France is taking the first decisive step in the construction of Europe, and associating Germany with it. Conditions in Europe will, as a result, be entirely transformed. This transformation will make possible other joint action which has been impossible until now.
> First of all, Europe will be born, a Europe solidly united and strongly built. A Europe whose standard of living will rise through the pooling of the production and the broadening of markets, which will lead to a lowering of costs. A Europe where the Ruhr, the Saar and the nearby regions of France will work together and enable their peaceful work [...] to benefit all Europeans, East and West, without discrimination [...].'

Schuman turned the page. Then, in his rather dull, gruff voice, he read the text of the proposal. So unfamiliar was it that toward the end he missed a sheet. But Monnet's team made sure that the press had copies:

> World peace can only be safeguarded by creative efforts which match the dangers that threaten it [...] Europe

will not be built all at once or as a single whole; it will be built by concrete achievements which first create de facto solidarity. The gathering together of European nations requires that the age-old opposition between France and Germany must be eliminated [...]. To this end the French Government proposes immediate action on a limited but decisive point: to place the whole of French-German coal and steel production, under a common High Authority, in an organization open to the participation of the other countries of Europe [...].

The solidarity in production thereby achieved will make it plain that any war between France and Germany becomes not only unthinkable but materially impossible. The establishment of this powerful unity of production [...] will lay the real foundation for their economic unification [...].

By the pooling of basic production and the establishment of a new High Authority whose decisions will be binding on France, Germany and the others which join them, this proposal will achieve the first concrete bases of the European Federation which is indispensable to the maintenance of peace [...].

The principles and essential commitments described above will be the subject of a treaty signed by the States and submitted for ratification by the Parliaments.

When Schuman finished speaking, one reporter asked him if what he was proposing was not a leap into the unknown. 'Exactly,' Schuman answered, 'a leap into the unknown.' Europe was to renounce the law of the jungle; its nations were to become fellow-citizens in a civilized community.

It was a turning point in European history. One odd token of it stuck in Monnet's mind. 'Do you remember André?' he asked me years later. 'He was our *maître d'hôtel* [butler and driver] at that time. He was with me for thirty years. Well, when we made the Schuman Plan it was all done very much behind the scenes. André knew nothing about it. And on the day the declaration came out, he heard the news on the radio. He came to see me and said "You'll never eat off the same plates again." It was a *maître d'hôtel*'s reaction. But he was right. Everything was changed.'

When the press conference was over, an usher approached one of the reporters, David Schoenbrun of the Columbia Broadcasting System. 'Would he please come along the corridor to the foreign minister's office?'

> The usher opened the door and I walked in to see three familiar faces, smiling at me, from the deep, red-silk armchairs of the minister's baroque bureau: the thin fox-like face of Pierre Uri, one of France's most brilliant political scientists and economists; the square, freckled, confidence-inspiring face of Etienne Hirsch, once a chemical engineer but now the top brain-truster of 'the Plan,' France's re-equipment and modernization ministry, and, between the two, the shrewd, mandarin-like countenance of the High Priest of the Plan, Commissioner General Jean Monnet.

Early that evening, Monnet told Schoenbrun: 'This Community of Coal and Steel that we have proposed is only the beginning. It must and will be extended to other areas [...] until someday a United States of Europe will emerge [...]. As Clement Attlee, the British Premier, put it, Europe must "federate or perish."'

This phrase of Attlee's, spoken in 1949, was to mislead and disappoint continental Europeans as much as Churchill's words in Zurich three years earlier. There had always been a fatal ambiguity in British use of the word 'Europe'; did it include Britain or not? When Ernest Bevin, for example, had proposed a 'United States of Europe' at the Trades Union Congress in 1927, he had almost certainly thought of Britain as standing outside.

Three years later he had advised against British membership in 'a European block.' Now as foreign secretary, Bevin resisted all efforts to make the OEEC or the Council of Europe a basis for unity rather than mere cooperation.

The father of Europe

In this, Bevin was not alone. Both Britain's major political parties at that time shared similar assumptions. Both seem convinced that Britain's wartime status made her unique in peacetime; that the Commonwealth could be a power-base like the Empire; that there was still a 'special relationship' with the United States. Both were unwilling to believe that Britain now resembled her nearest neighbours, small and relatively weak unless they acted together. Both were suspicious of continental rhetoric and both distrusted attempts to set long term goals.

The Labour Party, in particular, felt uneasy with the Christian-Democrats governments of France, Germany and Italy as a 1950 party memorandum stated: Any union with Europe entailing the least surrender of sovereignty must, unless all participating European government have similar socialistic economies, be a potential threat to [...] this country.' It had not yet become clear that Britain's dependence on foreign trade and capital made it impossible to insulate her economy. Only a few isolated idealists in the party realized as early as 1950 that unity in Europe could contribute both to Britain's own prosperity and to world peace.

***

On the morning of May 9, 1950, while the French cabinet had still not approved Schuman's proposal, Dean Acheson left Paris for London. When he arrived, the news had still not reached the Foreign Office so he said nothing to his luncheon host, Foreign Secretary Bevin. During lunch, a message arrived from the French ambassador asking for an appointment with Bevin that afternoon. As Acheson realized, it was to announce the Schuman Plan but he still felt bound to keep the secrecy exacted from him by the French.

At 4 pm, when they met again, Bevin asked to see him alone. 'He was in a towering rage, and at once charged that I had known of Schuman's plan and kept it from him. He rushed on to accuse me of having conspired with Schuman to create a European combination against British trade with the continent.' Bevin had politely told the French ambassador that when the British government saw the proposal's details it would examine them with great care but that in the meantime he could make no comment.

In reality, as Acheson put it 'he bristled with hostility to Schuman's whole idea.' The abruptness of the French announcement had irritated the British but fundamental decisions of foreign policy spring from deeper roots than irritation. Sir Kenneth Younger, minister of state at the foreign office, noted 'a nation-wide attitude which could not be doubted'– a visceral reluctance to get involved.

Richard Mayne's account of the Schuman role, based on Dean Acheson's recollections, omits the September 1949 Washington talks of Acheson, Bevin and Schuman when the last-named was pressed by his colleagues to come to London the next May with a solution to the 'German Problem'. Schuman took this charge seriously for the next nine months with the key contribution of Monnet to the idea of the Schuman Plan. If recalled and presented by Acheson in London, Bevin's anger might have been mitigated.

Acheson also misunderstood the source of Monnet's initiative with the Schuman Plan. The secretary of state attributes it to a reaction to a speech given in April 1950 by Prime Minister Georges Bidault seeking an Atlantic council. (See Dean Acheson, Present at the Creation, New York, 1969 382-386; JMM 299-305 and the Bernard Clappier's oral history in FJME cited earlier).

'I can still see the face of my friend Ernest Bevin' wrote Schuman twenty years later. 'To him it seemed impossible, unthinkable, that for an English man, for an English Government, there should be any authority set above the British Parliament. No argument could shake this position, not because of any kind of obstinacy – the Englishman is capable of great empirical flexibility – but as a result of logical reasoning [...]. At the beginning we were not perhaps sufficiently aware of that fact, which is why were under the illusion that we could secure British membership right away.'

The first British press comments encouraged this view. Only the Daily Express and the Communist Daily Worker were unfriendly to the Schuman Plan – a conjunction of the right wing and extreme left opposition that become almost traditional. Except for *The Economist,* however, most papers treated the Plan as economic rather than potentially political, and few called for Britain to join it. Speaking for many, the weekly Statist urged that she 'wait and see.'

But Monnet was anxious to get things moving. On May 10 he sent a copy of the declaration to Sir Edwin Plowden. The next day saw two encouraging statements, both from London. One was from Acheson who welcomed the Schuman Plan as 'a most important development [...] [to further] rapprochement between Germany and France and progress toward the economic integration of Western Europe.' The second, perhaps a little more guarded, was from the British Prime Minister, Clement Attlee, speaking in the House of Commons:

> It is the declared policy of the Western Powers to promote the entry of Germany as a free member into the comity of European nations. The French proposals are designed to facilitate that process... as a notable contribution.
> The proposals also have far reaching implications for the future economic structures of participating countries; this will require very careful study by His Majesty's government and the other governments concerned.

On May 12, the *London Times* published a collective letter urging the British government to accept the Schuman Plan. Its signatories included many prominent political figures including future prime minister Harold Macmillan and Arthur Salter, both friends of Monnet. On the same day, Anthony Eden made a speech at Warwick in which he welcomed the Schuman Plan.

All this made Monnet hopeful when he came to London two days later for talks with Plowden, other British officials and American leaders John McCloy and Charles Bohlen. Schuman, meanwhile, had already begun discussing the project with Bevin and Chancellor Sir Stafford Cripps in the intervals of the foreign ministers' conference.

In these conversations, the British raised questions and doubts. What would be the position of cartels? Might the Schuman Plan depress the standard of living? How would it affect French planning? Would it affect the ownership of industry? What form would the proposed High Authority have? Would it have the power to close down mines or steelworks? What relationship would it have with the national governments? And what about the United States position? Would the Plan not encourage American isolationism? Finally, how would the Eastern Powers react? Might the Schuman Plan not solidify the 'cold war'?

To the British, such questions seemed natural: they were astonished to find how little concrete detail the Plan yet contained. As Plowden told Monnet toward the end of his stay, 'the British wanted a piece of paper, never mind if that paper is a document, an example, a suggestion so long as it is a piece of paper.' To meet this request, Monnet asked Hirsch and Uri to draw up a series of questions and answers about the Schuman Plan. It declared, among other things:

> A through study has been made in Paris of the main questions raised by the proposal. Deliberately however, the French government mentioned in its proposals only those ideas which seem essential to achieve an effective construction rapidly. Everything that is not formally provided for is left open to discussion, and all solutions can be examined in depth.

Monnet, in other words, saw questions of detail as secondary; to tackle them first, before agreeing on the objective, might well prove fatal to the Plan. This looked, superficially, like the stereotype of continental dogmatism versus British pragmatism but there was both flexibility and rigidity on both sides. The British were as rigid in adhering to the unspoken doctrine of national sovereignty as

Monnet was in contesting it, while Monnet was unfailingly pragmatic in leaving concrete measures to be adopted later. What the British saw as a natural reluctance to sign a blank cheque seemed to the interlocutors a refusal to take a stake in a new company whose future trading results could not be known in advance. It was a pattern of mutual behaviour that marked Britain's relations with her European partners for years to come.

In the Spring of 1950, however, it was especially important to be firm. For Monnet, the Schuman Plan was a unique opportunity to begin changing international relations by establishing in Europe and in a limited field, rules and institution binding equally on all the participating governments. In the past, Britain had successfully resisted any such progress; as if instinctively, she had emasculated both OEEC and the Council of Europe. It was all the more important now to commit her to the common objective lest in discussing the means she lead others – above all, Germany – to forsake the ends.

And if she refused that commitment? At one time, a British refusal might have blocked the project: but this was no longer so. On May 15, at the Anglo-French press luncheon, Schuman had declared that France 'would pursue the project with only one other country if necessary.' Monnet himself was convinced that Britain, always a realist, would adjust to the facts.

Looking back later, Monnet remarked: 'I think the British are not open to ideas – no, that's too strong – they resist ideas. But they don't resist facts. And I was convinced that if the British did not come to us at that moment, they would come later when we had succeeded. But we had to prove it [...].'

Monnet left London on May 19. Shortly after, he went with Clappier to meet Adenauer for the first time to put the French proposal formally to him. But first, he had to ensure the agreement of the Allied control commission which, with its American, British and French members, ruled occupied West Germany. He explained the project and proposed to call on Adenauer to open negotiations. The commission as a whole was in agreement but some of its members thought that it should take part in the talks. 'This I refused,' Monnet said afterwards 'for a very simple reason. I said to the commission "There will be a negotiation if France and Germany sit as equals round the table without supervision of any kind." Finally, everyone agreed with this point of view.'

That afternoon, Monnet called on Adenauer, who had Blankenhorn with him. Adenauer found Monnet 'a man of very great talent for economic organization, a sure man of peace, a man with winning ways of negotiating. Then and later, we always remained close friends.' Monnet felt equally at ease with Adenauer 'The same relations were established between us,' he said, 'as between myself and Schuman – that is, friendship.'

Explaining the French government's thinking, Monnet argued that if technical experts were called in to negotiate it they would find and magnify countless difficulties. That would only endanger the whole project. What he proposed, therefore, was that the negotiating conference begin in Paris on June 20 but that in place of technical experts the participants should be people of some standing with a broad economic background and, above all, an ability to think in European rather than national terms. They should also be able to draft and discuss international treaties. The conference should proceed as quickly as possible and technical experts called in only afterwards when basic agreement had been reached on the mandate of the High Authority and the general shape of the treaty and when the national parliaments had given their broad approval.

Adenauer quickly agreed with this basic approach. Monnet then described the results of his London visit. 'The British,' he said, 'had in some respects shown themselves a little hesitant. But there was no need to worry. The British had the great virtue of being realistic, if the project succeeded, they would certainly rally round it,' Adenauer answered that he 'hoped Britain would understand her European role. To tell the truth, he did not doubt it; but the

British were people who needed to be given a little time.' After a brief first meeting with Ludwig Erhard, the minister of economic affairs, Monnet and Clappier returned to Paris.

Despite his reassuring words to Adenauer, Monnet was still anxious to allay British fears; and on May 25 he sent a long and careful letter to Sir Edwin Plowden. Three questions, he said, seemed to worry the British: What guarantees could be given against wrong or arbitrary decisions by the proposed High Authority? How would it fit in with, and assist, full employment and higher living standards? And how would it act with governments and firms?

The High Authority's independence from governments and interested parties, said Monnet, in reply to his own question, was the precondition for arriving at an overall European view which neither governments nor firms nor intergovernmental committees were capable of taking. The High Authority would, of course, consult with governments, industrialists, trade unionists and experts of all kinds. Its charter would also be negotiated by governments and ratified by parliaments. Further, there would be means of appeal.

Apart from its duty to eliminate discrimination, Monnet added, the High Authority's task would not require it to take the place of governments or to impose decisions on them. Instead its role would be to persuade them to take steps whose choice would be up to them. He stressed that many changes could be made when negotiations began and after the High Authority principle was accepted.

On the same day Monnet wrote, the French government sent London a memorandum announcing that the federal German government had agreed to negotiate on the Schuman Plan and had accepted a draft communiqué that declared:

> The Governments of _____ are resolved to carry out a common action aiming at peace, European solidarity and economic and social progress by pooling their coal

and steel production and by the institution of a new High Authority whose decisions will bind the countries which will adhere to it in the future. Negotiations on the basis of the principles [...] [of 9 May will open shortly] with a view to drawing up a Treaty which will be submitted for ratification to the respective Parliaments.

This draft text, the memorandum added, had been sent to the Belgian, Dutch, Luxembourg and Italian governments. The French government hoped that Britain would also be able 'to participate on the same conditions [...] from the outset.'

Monnet hoped that his letter to Plowden, together with the news that France and Germany were bent on action and had proposed it to other European countries, would now tip the British toward participation. But for once the British were too quick for him. By an unhappy coincidence, his letter and the French memorandum crossed with a message from London sent the same day. In this, Bevin rejected the idea of a 'full scale international conference' based on 'a prior commitment of principle.' He proposed, instead,

direct conversations between France and Germany in which the British would like 'to participate from the outset, with the hope that, by obtaining a clearer picture of how the proposals would operate, they would be able to join this scheme.'

When Sir Oliver Harvey, the British ambassador in Paris, delivered that message to the French foreign office, its recipients were perplexed. Britain's desire to take part in the 'conversations' and her hope of joining the 'scheme' seemed encouraging but she made no mention of the basic principle and failed, in a probably inspired comment by Agence France Presse, 'to take account of a whole series of clarifications on the part of the French.' For the moment, Monnet advised patience; perhaps his own letter and the French memorandum would modify the British position. They did – but not on fundamentals.

A further Bevin note declared that if the French government insisted on a 'commitment to pool resources and set up an authority with certain sovereign powers as a prior condition' his government would be unable to accept such a condition and would greatly regret such an outcome.

Behind the guarded diplomatic language of a subsequent British memorandum soon after, it was easy to sense irritation. Monnet's and Schuman's initiative looked like an effort to rush the British into an ominous and cloudy scheme for 'pooling resources' and to do so by rapidly recruiting other countries that were either much smaller than France or Britain, or had only lately emerged from defeat.

From Monnet's viewpoint, those embarking on the negotiations should agree on what they were about. This by no means meant that every participant would thereby be committing in advance to pooling resources under the High Authority; only the eventual treaty could pledge to do that. What was in question was a commitment of purpose. Were the British afraid of being enticed further than they now intended? Were they over- anxious to avoid raising false hopes? Or, might they, after further explanation, agree to negotiate on the basic proposal, then find that what they had feared turn out to be acceptable after all?

It was a meagre hope; but it seemed worth a trial. French ambassador Massigli called on Kenneth Younger, the British minister of state. 'He asked me,' Younger reported:

> [if] while we are not prepared to commit ourselves now to the principle of pooling resources under an international authority possessing sovereign powers, we are not taking an attitude of opposition to this principle but are prepared to [find] a practical method of applying the principle.
> I told him that I thought that roughly expressed the difference [...]. The Ambassador said he had always felt sure

that this was our attitude [...]. He said he found my explanation reassuring since it seemed to him that our reservations would not [...] limit our effective participation.

Massigli, in private, had serious reservations about the plan and objected to Schuman about the way in which Monnet and the Foreign Minister had launched it. 'You've smashed the china... and you expect me to mend it.'

Whether the British government had by now determined to opt out, Monnet made one last monumental effort of persuasion. With the help of Hirsch and Uri, he drafted a brief explanation of the plan which Schuman handed to Harvey. He pointed out that previous British Notes seemed to have misunderstood the commitment to principle. This was no debating quibble; at that moment it still seemed possible that semantics, not politics, separated Britain and France.

If Monnet remained hopeful, however, Robert Schuman was by now beginning to have doubts. While they waited for a further British response, the Dutch government agreed to the communiqué proposed by the French government but added one reservation:

> '[S]ince this text implies the acceptance of certain principles which form the basis of the French Government's Memorandum, the Dutch government is obliged to reserve the right to retract during [...] negotiations, its acceptance of these principles [...] if [they] prove impossible in practice.'

Superficially, this appeared to confirm and justify Britain's own reservation. In reality, it did the reverse. Unlike the British, the Dutch accepted the aim of the negotiations. It merely made explicit the right of withdrawal which the most recent French note had stressed as available to any participant, including Britain. The question was: would Britain be prepared to follow the Dutch lead?

The answer finally came. It was still no. The British proposal added a paragraph to the draft communiqué, making clear its separate position:

> The United Kingdom will participate in [...] a constructive spirit and in the hope that [...] there will emerge a scheme which they will be able to join. But they cannot at this stage enter into any more precise commitment.

Monnet's feelings on reading this obtuse reply can easily be imagined. In the British draft, even the proposed negotiations had become mere 'conversations'; and British unwillingness to undertake even the 'commitment' to an objective. Worse still, the British were once again asking for a special status different from all other States. Experience in the International Ruhr Authority, OEEC and the Council of Europe had already shown how persistently the British endeavoured to dilute, divert and, if necessary, sabotage all attempts to go beyond ad hoc cooperation between nations.

It was not malice; it was seldom open hostility, rather it seemed to be a lack of imagination, an instructive stubbornness, a half-conscious habit and occasional indignant fear. Behind it lay a sense of national difference verging on a sense of superiority. Britain, in fact, was implicitly rejecting what lay at the root of the Schuman proposal: equality. Monnet saw the danger of doing so... especially as regards Germany. On June 1 he pointed out in a confidential note to the French government:

> [...] if Britain takes part in the negotiations in such a way that she is able not to propose but to dispute the principles themselves, other countries will do the same. To accept British participation on these terms is therefore to resign oneself [...] to the replacement of the French proposal by a conception which would only be a travesty of it.

Monnet's note was nicely calculated to appeal to French national sentiment rather than to any suspect idealism. But ever now he was still not prepared to give up. That same day, the French government made one last effort by changing several key phrases to put the point to the British in a form they might accept.

But Schuman made clear in the note that time was running out. In fact, the British government had set up an interdepartmental committee headed by Plowden to prepare 'proposals inspired by the French initiative of 9th May'. AFP reported that these would be submitted at or after the opening of the Schuman Plan conference where the British hoped to maintain 'an invisible presence.' The proposals were never presented but they were radically different from the Schuman Plan and entirely technical rather than political.

On June 13, the Labour Party produced a notorious pamphlet, misleadingly titled *European Unity*. While paying lip service to Schuman's 'historic proposal,' it expressly rejected its basic aim. What reactions Monnet would have had if the British proposals went to the Plan conference became clear two months later when his friend, Harold Macmillan, put forward similar ideas from the Conservative side.

Macmillan, who a decade later was to lead Britain to the threshold of the European Community, had told the House of Commons in 1948 that 'Europe needs a common currency [and] a free movement of goods [...].' The next year he proposed to the Council of Europe that its ministers 'shall be an executive authority with supranational powers.' In May 1950 he had deplored 'the somewhat tepid reception given so far [...] to the Schuman proposals.'

Shortly after the Labour pamphlet, Macmillan sent an urgent private note to Churchill urging him to press the government into negotiating on Schuman's proposals. 'Britain should be in from the start – then we can mould the plan to our own pattern.'

With broad support from other Conservatives, this gave a clue to the counter-proposals which Macmillan submitted to the Council of Europe in August 1950. Any member country could form a ministerial committee which, in turn, would appoint an Authority for coal and steel. The basic principles would be intergovernmental: each country would have a veto and the right to withdraw.

Macmillan sent a copy of his plan to Monnet in advance. When it was made public in Strasbourg, Monnet wrote a long letter back, thanking him for the opportunity to comment. But it was misleading, he wrote, in part to refer to its proposals as versions of the Schuman Plan 'which are revolutionary or they are nothing.'

So ended Jean Monnet's third unsuccessful attempt, after 1940 and 1949, to initiate something more than mere cooperation with Great Britain. In view of Macmillan's later role, a most appropriate epitaph was his speech to the CE Assembly that same month. In it, he said, Monnet

> has made certain proposals and no one has greater respect for [him] than I have. He knows as much as any man about the peculiar problems which confront the British in these affairs. He longs for permanence; he knows the British like a trial run. The French have a saying that only the provisional endures [...]. [I]n the huge tasks which await us [...] we shall need many provisional arrangements. To meet this crisis [...] we British will certainly be prepared to accept the merging of sovereignty in practice if not in principle.

In 1975, Monnet said in a BBC interview that in 1950 'when we began the getting together of the nations of Europe, the difficulties...were great but also the temptation to get together was great. France and Germany got together. Their union was natural...I think they realized that to improve their conditions...they had to act together. They had known occupation, humiliation, defeat. All of this you [Britain] have not known. Why is it Britain, who is so practical, should not join this organization of Europe? Why? When it is so obviously in her own interest? I think this is the price of victory. We [Europeans] finished the war with a realization that we had to do something. We had to organize differently that we did before the war. You did not.'

Monnet added that this 'price of victory' [was] the illusion that you could maintain what you had without change.

Michael Charlton, the BBC journalist, was so impressed with Monnet's insight that he used it as the title of his book on post WWII British attitudes toward Europe, The Price of Victory *(London, 1983).*

Monnet was not in Strasbourg to hear the encouraging if premature words of Macmillan. For the past two months he had been busy with more immediate tasks. On June 20 the delegations of the Six had met...to begin negotiating on the Schuman Plan. Their first session was opened by Schuman himself in the Salon de l'Horloge where he had made his declaration on May 9. Then the negotiations began in earnest.

Monnet, as leader of the French delegation, was made chairman of the conference and he quickly marked it with his unorthodox methods. In the words of the official report 'the discussions did not have the traditional character [...] but of a constructive effort whose aim was not to eliminate disagreement but to solve the multitude of problems raised [...]. For the first time, the participating governments did not seek a provisional compromise [...] they took a common view of their common interest [to reach] the goal which they had recognized as valid for all of them.'

Inevitably there were elements of traditional bargaining especially toward the end, but the refreshing impact of Monnet's initial start was well described by Dutch delegate Max Kohnstamm, who later became one of his closest colleagues and friends:

> During the nine months that it took to turn the Schuman Declaration into a treaty [...] [h]e saw to it that neither the central objective, a European Community, nor the proposed method, delegation of powers to common institutions, got lost in the mass of details about coal, steel, scrap, transport, wages, cartels, distortions and discrimination.

The father of Europe

He showed great flexibility. The delegations were not confronted with French positions but were invited to discuss, to contribute, to help find common answers. Monnet never defended a merely national... partial view. Some of the delegates at first believed they were simply being tricked when... they saw Frenchmen disagreeing among themselves. How could one negotiate one's nation's special interests... if the inviting delegation seemed to have no clear view of the national interest it wanted to defend? But Monnet's method was so contagious...was so liberating and exhilarating that none of the delegates resisted this new approach for very long.

Monnet's German counterpart was Walter Hallstein, a shy, bespectacled Rhinelander, brilliant lawyer and former rector of Frankfurt University. In 1958 he would become the first president of the newly formed Commission of the European Economic Community. The chief Dutch delegate, Dirk Spierenburg, was likewise to become vice president of the Schuman Plan's High Authority.

At a more technical level, Monnet's deputy at the French Plan, Etienne Hirsch, headed a group which included men who became senior high authority officials. Pierre Uri's fertile brain and pen were omnipresent and from time to time Monnet consulted outside lawyers who later became court of justice leaders.

The Paris negotiating conference was the start of what became known as the 'Monnet grapevine,' an informal, European network of information and influence which largely ignored national, institutional or hierarchical boundaries.

Instead of producing a draft treaty to be examined, haggled over, amended and eventually initialled, Monnet put forward a 'working document' in eleven main sections, expanding on the broad principles of the Schuman Declaration. The aim was 'a partial merger of sovereignty' beyond coal and steel, to lay 'the foundations for a European Community.' *[See JMM 296 for more on the political goals of the Schuman Plan.]*

The document proposed that the High Authority should have relatively few members appointed jointly by the governments and that none should have a direct mandate from any national government. The High Authority should be responsible to – and subject to dismissal by – a 'Common Assembly' elected by and from the national parliaments. Thus, his working documents explained, 'the very parliaments which would have abandoned part of their sovereignty would be partially merged to exercise it jointly.'

This last suggestion not only answered the reproach that the High Authority would be beyond democratic control; it also made ever clearer the political implications of what some still might think as technical questions. A number of the delegates left the first session saying that they had not realized the full scope of the negotiations and that they needed to consult their governments.

When they met again in July, the Belgian and Dutch participants proposed to complete the Schuman Plan's central framework of High Authority, Court and Assembly with a fourth institution, the Council of Ministers. As first, Monnet was wary of the idea. The essence of the Schuman Plan, after all, was deliberated transnational interpenetration, the knitting together of separate economies, the gradual achievement of a united Europe. It would be fatally easy to relapse from this difficult task into the familiar pattern of limited cooperation through intergovernmental or diplomatic routines between separate states.

But he recognized, as the French delegation's official report put it, that 'there could be no question of artificially isolating the member States coal and steel production, 'declaring it supranational and setting up institutions to deal with it irrespective of the general economy of the member States. It was therefore necessary to provide for a link.'

This was the 'special' Council of Ministers whose task in the eventual treaty 'was to harmonize the action of the High Authority and that of the governments' – very modest when compared with the central role that the Council was to assume as economic integration proceeded. For extreme or doctrinaire 'supranational-ity' but not for Monnet himself, this 'special' Council of Ministers was a little cloud out of the sky, like a man's hand.

The ultimate shape of the coal and steel community's institutions was not settled until much later. Negotiations lasted throughout 1950 and into early 1951. Along the way, technical problems arose – disquiet of French steelworkers worried about the high cost of Belgian coal mines, concern over Italy's perennial shortage of raw materials, German and other's suspicions about the 'dirigistic' [interventionist] nature of the High Authority.

As months went by, however, Monnet's persuasiveness and sense of urgency, supported by the conciliatory tact of Robert Schuman, smoothed most problems away. By December 1950, much of the draft treaty was completed but disagreement persisted over con-trolling mergers and dismantling cartels. The main objections came from the German steel industry. In October both Hallstein and Adenauer had to reaffirm backing for the Schuman Plan but they faced increasing opposition at home.

Not for the first time, Monnet turned to his American friends for help. During the Winter of 1950-51, David Bruce and John McCloy, assisted by McCloy's general counsel, Robert Bowie, became vir-tual participants in the negotiations, finally overcoming the last of the objections in February. In March the draft treaty was initiated. Monnet then went to Bonn for two days of last minute talks with Hallstein and Adenauer.

Germany, he learned, was about to proposed that each country's voice in the Community's institutions be proportional to its pro-duction of coal and steel. This would have given Germany the dominant role. Instead Monnet insisted that France and Ger-many should have equal voting rights in both the Council and the Assembly. Adenauer agreed.

In April the foreign ministers of the Six gathered again in Paris to sign the treaty of the first European community. The first draft had 95 articles; by now Monnet's 'brain trust' had stretched it to a full one hundred. A further symbolic touch: the document itself was printed in French by the National Printing Office in German ink, on Dutch vellum, bound in Belgian parchment with Italian ribbon and Luxembourg glue. The pooling of the Community resources had already begun.

It would take a further 15 months to complete ratification in the six parliaments. Not until August 1952 was the European Coal and Steel Community a tangible reality. By that time Jean Monnet had already been engaged for nearly two years on a further European venture whose fortunes were to prove very different from those of the first.

The Pleven Plan

The Schuman Plan conference had been at work for less than a week when Europe was suddenly gripped by the fear of war.

At dawn on June 25 1950, North Korean troops crossed the 38th Parallel and invaded the South. Summoned by the United States, the United Nations Security Council called for a cease-fire but this was ignored. The next day, President Harry S Truman promised aid and supplies to South Korea and then ordered General MacArthur to give naval and air support. Undeterred, the North Korean forces pressed on and by June 28 had occupied Seoul, the southern capital.

The Security Council condemned North Korea's breach of the peace and recommended that the UN supply the Republic of Korea the help necessary to repulse the armed attack and re-establish peace and security. Before long, America and her allies were engaged in real if limited hostilities.

The weakness of Europe's conventional defence might in more normal times have been offset by a greater American effort. Britain and the Netherlands were already spending on defence a higher proportion of their national income than the United States and France only a little less. But the United States was now committed to the Korean War; and, far from increasing its contribution to the defence of Europe, it was seeking European help. In July 1950, the Brussels Pact powers agreed to increase armaments and to prolong military service but the scope for further effort was limited.

Charles de Gaulle, from his political exile, gave the idea of a unified European army his backing. Following Konrad Adenauer denunciation of any German 'mercenary' army, he proposed instead a real German force within a European army. In August, Winston Churchill proposed, at the Council of Europe's Assembly, 'the creation of a unified European Army subject to proper European democratic control…' His motion was carried 89 to 5 with 27 abstentions.

Fear and suspicion multiplied, however, when the same month, President Truman asked the Allies how Europe could improve its military arrangements. Although he avoided mentioning Germany, it was very clear what was on his mind.

Jean Monnet had been at Houjarray discussing the Schuman Plan [with, among others, long-time American advisor George Ball] when news of the Korean conflict came. Now he was quick to react to Truman's inquiry busy as he was with the Schuman Plan conference, he prepared a draft reply on behalf of the French government, now headed by his friend and former assistant, René Pleven with Robert Schuman still foreign minister.

Characteristically, Monnet's rather reluctant approach to defence was from the starting point of pooling resources and supplies. France, his draft declared, was ready to participate without reservation in the common defence of the West. The Western countries had enough economic, human and financial resources but they were inefficiently used. He proposed 'a common fund to centralize and administer in the most efficient way the greatest possible proportion of the resources devoted by each country to defence', i.e. a joint procurements fund, deriving its revenue from weighted national contributions, international taxes and collective loans.

At this stage, Monnet's proposals had little success. The French response to Truman referred in vague terms to 'a collective effort'; but it did not seek formal acceptance of this principle, nor did it propose any immediate action.

One step that he thought should be taken at once was to maintain enough troops in West Germany to prevent any putsch engineered from the East, similar to that in Korea. Another, in the slightly longer term, was to draw up French and European 'balance sheets' showing what armaments would be available by 1951, what more would be needed and what demands would be placed on raw materials, finance and other resources.

Monnet put these conclusions, including estimates of what defence efforts France could make without endangering her civil investments, in a note to Pleven. He suggested the budget be rigorously pruned to avoid duplication of Allied efforts. A week later he drafted for Pleven another note to point out how France's Indo-China effort had weakened her position in Europe. But he was unsatisfied with the draft and never sent it.

He was in fact feeling uncharacteristically gloomy, perhaps the result of overwork. He was only 61 but that Spring and Summer he had not only run the French Plan but also launched the Schuman Plan, negotiated with the British as well as worrying his way toward a new venture in European defence. Meanwhile the Council of Europe's Assembly voted something close to Macmillan's counter-proposals to the Schuman Plan.

Perhaps this was why, in late August, at his Ile de Ré vacation home, he wrote – partly in his own hand – an extraordinarily sharp and biting assessment of where Britain seemed to stand at this dangerous moment in history, and what must be done to build Europe. In retrospect, some of what he wrote seems exaggerated, unfair or mistaken; but some of it was perceptive:

- Britain has no confidence that France and other countries of Europe have the ability or even the will to resist a possible Russian invasion.
- Britain has little regard for the parliamentary democratic institutions of Europe.
- Britain believes that war is inevitable.
- Britain believes that in this conflict, continental Europe will be occupied but that she herself, with America, will be able to resist and finally conquer.
- She does not wish, if she can prevent it, that the other countries of Europe merge since this would handicap her freedom to maneuver and to act.
- We must avoid the error of [either] wanting to make Europe with Britain or against Britain.
- The United States has today effectively taken the place of Britain in political leadership; one cannot make [i.e. unite] continental Europe without the US.
- Everything that seeks to preserve the forms of the past is against this current. Everything that [seeks] a broader community [...] will move with this universal current and be enthusiastically received.

The forthcoming New York conference of British, French and US foreign ministers was bound to raise the question of German rearmament, he predicted. It was vital not to accept any solution counter to the Schuman Plan. Instead of sending a memo to Schuman, Monnet went to see him. Monnet's warnings proved prophetic.

In New York, Dean Acheson produced what was called 'the bombshell': America's take-it-or-leave-it proposal that NATO forces should include German divisions. Monnet was at home in Houjarray, slightly unwell, when news of Acheson's proposal reached

France. On reading the foreign ministers' final communiqué, he reacted quickly. He wrote Robert Schuman on the options regarding Germany:

> Three ways seem to be open: Do nothing? But is that possible? [Or] treat Germany on a national basis, but thereby make it impossible to build Europe and to succeed with the Schuman Plan; Or, integrate Germany in Europe through an enlarged Schuman Plan by taking in a European framework those decisions that will be taken.

When the NATO council met in September 1950, Schuman soon found that France was beginning to be isolated in her opposition to the US proposals. He cabled Paris for instructions, suggesting both 'Atlantic' and 'European' solutions. At the next meeting in October, the United States was expected to redouble pressure.

But there were signs of greater flexibility. France was reassured by US Defense Secretary George C. Marshall, that he would welcome a 'European defense proposal' from France, during the NATO Council meeting, if not earlier, Acheson learned of Monnet's plans. 'Why doesn't Schuman tell me so?' he asked Joseph Bech, the Luxembourg foreign minister. 'Because he doesn't know it yet,' Bech answered. But Bech was mistaken; a Schuman colleague told Acheson: 'Don't push Schuman so hard. He has to have time. We will work this out.'

In Paris, 'working this out,' was by now Monnet's main concern. He drafted and redrafted a series of notes to Schuman and Pleven. In them he warned that technical experts were getting bogged down in the Schuman Plan discussions, and forgetting that France's political goals were paramount. France's reluctance to see Germany rearmed was understandable but she could not prevent it because she needed American credits and American troops. Germany must share in the cost of Europe's defence.

Together with these notes, Monnet worked on successive drafts of a government statement. He proposed small military units of different nationalities, all wearing the same uniform. Germany should share in the planning, if not yet in the units' composition, from the start.

In preparing for the NATO meeting, Monnet and his colleagues worked more intensively still, drafting, discussing, redrafting and correcting. To win over French opposition, Monnet insisted more and more strongly on the dangers of a Germany growing more powerful without the restraints of the European Community.

He produced his final version of a government position paper. The next day, the Prime Minister presented the 'Pleven Plan' to increase the forces stationed in Europe and place them under a single supreme commander, with appropriate American financial and military aid. After three days of debate and hostile speeches from Communists and Gaullists, the French assembly approved the Pleven Plan 349 to 225.

To Jean Monnet, it looked as if the new European initiative had begun well. But elsewhere, the first reactions were hesitant. Soviet reaction to rearming Germany was predictably cool, with calls for renewing the Potsdam agreement on demilitarizing Germany. Britain and the United States seemed also hostile or at least hesitant.

Konrad Adenauer was also hesitant until a crucial talk with the French High Commissioner for Germany. He then called the Pleven Plan 'a considerable contribution to the integration of Europe' which did not discriminate against Germany.

Early in 1951, France invited all European NATO members, plus Germany to a negotiating conference on the Pleven Plan with the US and Canada as observers. When the parties met in Paris, there were hostile demonstrations. The crowds, like a Greek chorus, were an ominous sign.

When the Pleven Plan talks for the European Defence Community (EDC) began, Monnet was still busy with the 'Monnet Plan' at the rue de Martignac and with the final stages of negotiating the Coal and Steel Community treaty. Only when that treaty was signed in Spring 1951 could he devote more time to the EDC talks and by then the negotiating pattern had been set.

To say this is not to suggest than Monnet's absence caused EDC to fail. In background, he played an important part during at least 12 months of its fitful progress but the real difficulties were immense. Conceived in haste, the Pleven Plan was buried at leisure. It was certainly worth trying, but the opposition it aroused showed its hopes were slim.

In June 1951, the US High Commissioner for Germany, John McCloy, took to Washington the 'Petersberg Plan' worked out by Allied military experts at Petersberg, the seat of the Allied High Commission across the Rhine from Bonn. This provided for 12 German divisions to be integrated into NATO – the rearmament of Germany in the starkest form.

The Supreme Allied Commander, Dwight Eisenhower, initially did 'dislike the whole idea of a European Army. I had enough troubles without it', he wrote. But at the suggestion of McCloy, Monnet called on Eisenhower. It was eight years since their paths had crossed in Algiers but he managed to convince Eisenhower that it would be easier, safer and more effective to deal with one European Community than with separate European states. Out of their talks, then and later, grew a respect and affection ended only with their deaths.

The next day, Eisenhower sent a cable to Washington. After much thought, he concluded that the best and perhaps the only way to secure a German military contribution was to go ahead with a European Army based on equality and rights. If France was willing to play the game, the United States should work with it and give up the Petersberg negotiations which France had never accepted.

The shift in American policy had been radical and rapid and part of the responsibility for this belongs to Jean Monnet. But the consequences of this shift remained equivocal. Monnet's old friend, John Foster Dulles, who became secretary of state under President Eisenhower in January 1953, was a far less tactful man than his predecessor, Dean Acheson. It was Dulles who during WWII had gestured at a map of Europe behind Monnet's desk in the Willard Hotel in Washington and announced 'After the war all that will have to be united; otherwise nothing lasting can be built.'

It was Dulles again in December 1953 who threatened an 'agonizing reappraisal' of American policy toward Europe if France failed to ratify EDC. Looking back after EDC's final collapse the next year, many people were inclined to blame the United States for the excessive vehemence of its support; and part of that blame must also be borne by Monnet.

In 1951, however, the omens were still hopeful. Cooperation between British, French and American foreign ministers produced their support for a democratic Germany as an equal in the European Community. They described the Schuman Plan and the Pleven Plan as 'a great plan toward European unity,' and noted that Britain desired 'to establish the closest association with the European Community at every stage.' Changes in American policy had somewhat modified British policy also.

With this diplomatic progress, Monnet was free to turn back to the starting point of his concern for a European Army – the economic problems of Europe's common defence. To try to match needs and resources more fairly, France proposed at the NATO Council in Ottawa a method characteristic of Monnet: a committee of 'Three Wise Men' to draw up a 'balance sheet.'

Vociferous opposition arose, especially among the smaller powers. Eventually a compromise designated 'Twelve Apostles' with one member from each ally but with an executive bureau of three – the 'Wise Men' Averell Harriman, the chair, was joined by Sir Edwin Plowden and that master of the 'balance sheet' technique, Jean Monnet.

The report of this trio assigned specific financial obligations on the NATO members including Germany which was also praised for reconstructing a devastated country, resettling refugees and maintaining West Berlin. Monnet and his colleagues had made a first and fairly successful attempt to deal with a problem that was to dog the alliance for years to come.

Meanwhile the foreign ministers of the six countries negotiating the EDC met in Paris in early 1952 to recommend the broad outline of the treaty. Then the French Assembly held a crucial debate on the EDC. Robert Schuman's opening explanation was only moderately received. Several speakers deplored the absence of Britain and the inclusion of Germany. But finally on May 9, the 2nd anniversary of the Schuman Declaration, the heads of delegations at the EDC conference initialled the draft treaty. Schuman, Adenauer and their colleagues formally signed the EDC treaty in the Salon de l'Horloge of the French Foreign Ministry.

The Coal and Steel Community (ECSC)

Ratification of the Coal and Steel Treaty was nearly completed [by mid-1952]. Germany had been the first to finish the parliamentary procedure, followed soon by the other five countries. The first task proved easy. Jean Monnet was unanimously appointed the first president of the High Authority. More difficult were the questions of the working language and of the headquarters location.

Schuman had proposed French, the treaty language, but Adenauer – characteristically of the changing times – objected. French, German, Italian and Dutch were given equal status. In practice much of the work was done in French and some of it, unofficially, and increasingly, in English.

More difficult still was the Community's headquarters. Schuman proposed provisionally Strasbourg, site of the Council of Europe, then Saarbruecken when the Saar was 'Europeanized.' Belgium proposed Liege, the Netherlands suggested The Hague and Joseph

Bech, the stout, moustached, rather Chestertonian prime minister, foreign minister and wine minister of Luxembourg, proposed the Grand Duchy.

Discussion seemed endless. It was not even possible to agree on a provisional headquarters. With everyone exhausted, Bech stirred from somnolence that was possibly feigned. 'Since we have to start work somewhere, let me invite you to Luxembourg for our next meeting. After that, we'll see.' The High Authority and the Court of Justice started work in Luxembourg in August 1952; the Common Assembly would meet in Strasbourg a month later.

On August 11, 1952 the grey slate roofs of Luxembourg glittered in a blazing sun. 'That morning,' wrote François Fontaine, then Monnet's *chef de cabinet*, 'when the inhabitants woke they saw their city invaded by commandoes from five countries who had infiltrated during the night. Foreign cars drove across the Pont Adolphe at alarming speed. Strangers were taking over some public buildings. The Luxembourgers were no longer at home; they were in Europe.'

Monnet himself, now 63, led the first meeting of the High Authority in a château, mainly to make each other's acquaintance. Three of them had already worked together in the Schuman Plan conference: Dirk Spierenburg, the 43 years old Dutch delegate; and the plump but alert Albert Wehrer of Luxembourg. Joining them was the first Vice President, Franz Etzel, a tall, round headed, 49-year-old German who looked a typical 'Prussian.' In fact, he was from the Rhineland, warm hearted, deeply serious, easily moved.

The first High Authority meeting was brief. 'I think the journalists are waiting somewhere before lunch,' said Monnet. In all, there were 150 of them from all over Western Europe. They assembled that afternoon in the Town Hall. 'For the first time,' Monnet declared

> Traditional relations between states are being transformed. Traditionally, even European states are convinced

of the need to get together [...] [but] they retain[ed] their full national sovereignty [...]. Today, on the contrary, six parliaments have decided to establish the first European Community which is merging part of its members' national sovereignty [...] to the common interest.

It was almost an attack from the throne. In it emerged some of Monnet's characteristic ideas: that of a balance sheet, that of bringing together all interested parties, that of immediate concrete efforts... toward more ambitious progress in broader fields.

But the essential point, which Monnet saw, was the break with the past that the High Authority represented. Without it to act as a ploughshare, the long spectacular but far more extensive role of the later European Community [and European Union] might never have been possible.

After the opening came the work. Knowing that 'only provisional solutions last,' Albert Wehrer quietly arranged for part of the Luxembourg railways headquarters, an old rusticated brownstone building, to be allocated to the new Community. It was here, in a somber décor of cream-painted walls and brown linoleum, that the High Authority met on that August Monday morning at 10am. There were no flowers and no formal speeches, but practical decisions to be made.

Various members of the High Authority put forward plans for dividing up its activities. Without fuss, Monnet quietly shelved them all. 'We are a collective body,' he insisted. 'We have collective responsibility. Everyone must know all the problems we face.'

Equally, he refused a large administration. No bureaucrat himself, he distrusted formal organizations and well-defined jobs. What was important, in his view, was to maintain a small, flexible, politically responsible team. Typical was his recruiting method. Only when the basic commando groups were finally in control did he give in to pressure for more staff and more orthodox procedures.

Not until long after Monnet left the High Authority did its staff acquire established status; for years most of the original team was only on renewable contracts.

Veterans of the Luxembourg adventure tell many stories of his odd working methods. Officially the day began at 8:45am but Monnet might start at 6am with phone calls from his country home at nearby Bricherhof. Then he would take his morning walk in the woods. At 10am he might arrive at the office and call together his 'brain trust.' Work might go on, sustained only by sandwiches, until early afternoon. Then Monnet might on some days call a halt. 'We're not on form today – let's go for a walk.' At 5pm they would start again and often work to late in the evening, stopping for an hour, and only breaking up after midnight. Completely free weekends were rare.

It seemed chaotic and was sometimes unnecessary but it certainly worked. Monnet instilled his own sense of almost wartime urgency into people of very different nationalities and backgrounds, conflicting political philosophies and divergent attitudes and tastes. And because many came from business, industry, banking, academic life or political activity, they were innovators and 'fixers', not administrators. If they lacked civil service experience, they had rather eagerness and drive.

When I myself went to Luxembourg, almost the first official I saw was François Duchêne climbing into his ground floor office through the window to save himself a walk. Several senior officials, like Monnet, did much of their work in rough clothes at home.

Being in Luxembourg was an additional advantage. Small, landlocked and deeply traditional, the Grand Duchy offered few distractions, exerted little political pressure and in no sense overshadowed the nascent European Community. Busy, isolated, unafraid of local officialdom, the best of Monnet's team were attracted rather than irritated by the local life; the Letzeburgesch language, with its loan-words from French in an old-German context; the surrounding forests, the tiny theatre, the brass-band concerts on Sunday mornings. And if a few of the staff felt condescending toward their adopted home, this was an isolated outbreak of the complex that threatens all international officials, even in New York.

The basic task facing the High Authority was to remove the barriers to Community trade in coal and steel, to help build a strong economy and to improve both working conditions and the standards of living. It made a quick start on removing trade barriers, customs duties, quantitative restraints, dual prices, currency curbs and discrimination in transport rates. In February 1953 it opened the 'common market' for coal, iron ore and scrap.

Monnet took a personal hand in the proceedings. He travelled down to the Arbed steel works. There, as the NY Herald Tribune correspondent Don Cook described,

> A group of diplomats, politicians, civil servants and steel company executives and journalists gathered to watch one of those anticlimactic ceremonies by which great events are often set in motion. Jean Monnet, the 'Father of Europe,' had come to tap the first blast furnace to produce pig iron under the Coal and Steel Community.
> Arbed at the heart of Western Europe, for years had been producing steel from French ore, Belgian limestone, coking coal from Holland and Germany with a sprinkling of Italian workmen. In the molten pig iron bubbling inside that blast furnace, the six nations of Europe were already joined.

As economic integration proceeded, industrialists lost their original fear and suspicion of the ECSC. One important question still concerned relations with Britain. Failing British membership of the Community, the notion of some association with it had been mooted by Robert Schuman even during his London visit in May 1950. Now the new Conservative Government in Britain went a step further. When Winston Churchill and Anthony Eden had talks in Paris with René Pleven and Schuman in December 1951, their communiqué declared that Britain intended to establish close relations with the High Authority as soon as it was set up and to maintain a permanent delegation there. A few weeks later, however, a British staff proposal suggested that they scarcely understood what Monnet and his colleagues were trying to achieve.

Then, just months later, Foreign Minister Anthony Eden presented a proposal which came to be known as the 'Eden Plan' which sought to make the European Community a subdivision of the Council of Europe. The plan was not novel. Something like it had been suggested by Harold Macmillan nearly two years earlier in a counter-proposal to the Schuman Plan.

Deputies of the Council of Europe discussed the Eden plan at two lengthy meetings in April and May 1952. Their report noted the essential differences in structure between the Council of Europe and the European Community. The same day, Jacques Van Helmont, secretary to the French delegation at the ECSC conference, made the same points to Monnet. Soon thereafter, Paul Henri Spaak, the Belgian president of the Council of Europe Assembly, resigned in protest against the obstructionism shown by some members.

Behind some technical difficulties separating the two plans, there were political problems. What the Six were hoping to achieve was a pooling of resources and a fusion of material interests within a Community that would develop further as time went on. The Council of Europe, by contrast, was concerned with limited cooperation between sovereign states. Yet the Eden Plan seemed to ignore these differences.

In May the Council of Europe's ministers approved the Eden plan in principle. One week later its Consultative Assembly did likewise. But in the meantime Monnet got in touch with the Council of Europe to see what could be done reasonably under the protocol on relations with the Council signed by the ECSC members at the time the coal and steel treaty was signed. Even these provisions, however, seemed open to misunderstanding.

In July 1952, the Ministers of the Six agreed that their Common Assembly should hold its first meeting in the Strasbourg head-quarters of the Council of Europe. The council's secretary-general called on Monnet to discuss arrangements. Monnet pointed out, rather stiffly, that the ECSC Assembly was the first such body with sovereign powers. It could, for example, vote the High Authority out of office. His duty, he said, was to safeguard the assembly's independence. Its basic organization must therefore be quite distinct from the Council's Consultative Assembly. It must have its own secretariat. What Monnet wanted in fact was to borrow the building and its interpreters.

When the council's secretary-general resisted these moves, Monnet began to make alternative plans. He approached the tall and formidable Emile Blamont, secretary-general of the French Assembly, asking him to head a committee of colleagues from other national parliaments to organize the Common Assembly's first session. After explaining matters to his High Authority members, he wrote officially to the presidents of all six national parliaments, asking each to appoint a member to the preparatory committee.

The council's secretary-general countered with a plan of co-presidents which Monnet rejected. It was now Monnet's turn to be firm. 'We have only ten days. I am very sorry to have to dispense with your cooperation.' The council official backed down: 'I have no intention of maintaining a personal position' he told Monnet. The Common Assembly duly met for the first time in the Maison de l'Europe of the Council in September 1952. The European Parliament still meets there but now *[in the 1970s]* in a modern replacement which the Council later opened.

But if Monnet was suspicious of anything that threatened to 'drown' the new Community, he remained eager to bring Britain into the closest possible relationship with it. In August 1952 the British government announced in Luxembourg that it was ready to begin talks with the president of the High Authority.

Ten days later, Monnet went to London. The result was the British decision to send a permanent delegation to Luxembourg headed by Cecil Weir, a Scottish industrialist and civil servant. The United States announced that it would also send a permanent delegation headed by Monnet's friend, William Tomlinson *[from the Paris embassy]*.

Monnet then proposed that the Community should set up a 'Joint Committee' for the association with Britain. 'It would examine the questions we wish to deal with in common,' he wrote. The Joint Committee met the next month in Luxembourg with Weir and his senior staff as well as British coal and steel leaders from management and labour.

Soon the Eden plan died. By Spring 1953 the Coal and Steel Community had clearly emerged as an entity in its own right, no longer blurred or hampered by attempts, well-meaning as they seemed, to subordinate it to the Council of Europe. The whole sorry story looked like a farce, a storm in a civil-service teacup. But for Monnet and colleagues it involved a precarious principle. Now at last there were the beginnings of a European Community but its institutional structure was young and very fragile. 'Tragically,' commented a British minister, 'our initiative had only aroused suspicion that we were trying to sabotage the unity of Europe.' His remark was all too apt.

The link between the Six's common market for coal and steel and the Community's relations with Britain, as Monnet saw it, was much more than purely formal. What Monnet and his team had in mind was establishing institutions and procedures whereby Britain could gradually become more involved in the Community. During the remainder of 1953 and 1954, Monnet laboured to reach this association agreement. It was the kind of challenge he loved, especially since his day-to-day work was increasingly a predictable routine run by the expanding staff.

Meanwhile this initiative by the High Authority had to be explained to the member governments, some of whom felt that Monnet had stepped beyond his authority. In the middle of the next phase of negotiations, he fell ill. Much of the summer of 1954 he spent recovering from general fatigue---he was, after all, almost 66 years old but still worked like a man of 30. When he returned to his desk in September, he was no longer smoking the cigars he had enjoyed for so many years.

The High Authority's proposals should be submitted now to the British, Monnet believed. He outlined the approach to his colleagues:

> The association we envisage cannot be a common market [...]. We shall be concerned to decide what action can be taken in common with Britain in ways that do not involve abandonment of sovereignty.

Monnet's original ideas, it was clear, had undergone some transformation but behind the prudent wording the substance was potentially as ambitious. He still hoped for a pooling of markets, for joint action and common rules and institutions modeled indirectly on those of the Community. Weir acknowledged receiving these ideas in Monnet's letter and transmitted them to London.

Britain's first public reaction came in January 1954 when Anthony Eden answered a parliamentary question by saying the High Authority proposal would require careful study. This initial response seemed lukewarm. Monnet was ready to start official negotiations, but he still had to wait three months for Britain to respond. At last in late April 1954, Cecil Weir came to see him. He was smiling as he handed over the crucial letter. But its substance was only that Britain was ready to discuss the whole of relations with the Community, as Monnet's December letter had suggested.

After such mountainous labour, Monnet might have expected more. Had it really taken four months since his Christmas letter to reach so anodyne a formula? Whatever he felt, Monnet looked at the positive points: Association 'would be politically desirable [...] the government would like to examine the suggestions made'; it was inviting him to London.

When the Consultative Assembly of the Council of Europe met in late May, a British Member of Parliament said Britain could not abandon part of its national sovereignty. He warned Monnet that the British public was hesitant about a close association.

It was late in the evening when Monnet rose to reply. A journalist later noted that 'it was a real personal success.' In it he reviewed the prospects for association. He said his British colleague indicated some of the 'misunderstandings and ignorance' of the coal and steel community. 'My colleagues and I will travel to London to explore these problems.' But before that trip planned for the next month, Monnet fell ill. It was September before he could travel.

After several months of talks, the British promised to submit a more formal paper as soon as they could. Soon thereafter, two draft documents came from London. When Monnet and his team examined them, they were dismayed. What the British government was proposing was a very watered-down affair. A few subsequent British amendments seemed more positive. Months of talks followed.

Monnet's conduct of what amounted to secret negotiations with Britain was characteristic both of his own temperament and of his conception of the High Authority's role which he saw as something like a sovereign power, independent of national governments. But this view was not shared by every member government.

In the final months of 1954, he worked closely and constantly with his British counterpart, now Duncan Sandys, minister of supply and Churchill's son-in-law. Any agreement would have to be approved by the member governments and their parliaments but Monnet had gone a very long way toward the final text with no Community minister even being informed. It would be a delicate matter now to clear the draft through his Council of Ministers.

By the time the council met in November, many problems had been eliminated. The council accepted the text the next month only slightly revised from Monnet's draft. Shortly before Christmas, almost exactly one year after his draft had gone to Cecil Weir, the High Authority team of Monnet, Etzel and Spierenburg signed the final text in London with Sandys and the six ambassadors of the Community member states. It was ratified in February 1955 by Britain and went into effect in September.

The results of the Association Agreement were not spectacular. Britain cut coal exports in early 1956 which prompted the High Authority to call for consultations. Britain then reduced steel tariffs while the Community countries harmonized their's. This was still far from the common market in coal and steel Monnet has originally envisaged.

But the regular meetings, the growing habit of looking at problems together, and the discreet but intense diplomatic activity of the Community's London delegation all contributed to the gradual erosion of mutual ignorance and isolation. And if the agreement did not evolve into virtual membership, as Monnet had once hoped, this was certainly not any fault of his. In the ratification debate in the House of Commons, the Labour spokesman, Alfred Robens, paid Monnet a memorable tribute:

> I believe Jean Monnet to be a man of very great vision. He really believes in the economic integration of Europe. His goal is peace and prosperity [...]. Jean Monnet, who was the great architect of this work, deserves the highest tribute from all of us in European parliaments [...]. I believe that historians will write of Jean Monnet that he was essentially a man with a practical mind whose forward vision placed him [...] ahead of his fellow men.

The history of how Monnet negotiated Britain's association with the nascent European Community shows these qualities. It reveals, first and foremost, Monnet's persistence---his incessant daily efforts toward the same goal; surprising intransigence if the goal was endangered but equally surprising flexibility about the means. Secondly, Monnet's efforts witnessed his conviction that without Britain the Community would remain incomplete and his perpetual readiness to coax and cajole her out of her insular stance. Third, and most of all, Monnet refused to be diverted from the overall objective by either the details of his presidency of the High Authority or the daunting setbacks.

In the background of these humdrum negotiations, a larger drama was playing itself out to a conclusion which made the negotiators seem stoical. While Monnet was doing his best to build and extend the Coal and Steel Community, his 'Pleven Plan' for a European Defence Community was coming to grief. With its collapse came the first defeat also for fuller political integration.

The Relaunching

In the summer of 1952, when the High Authority had begun in Luxembourg, Sir Cecil Weir had travelled there to follow its work for Britain. The barometer had seemed to be set fair for further European integration. The treaty establishing a European Defence Community (EDC) had been signed in Paris in May; the Six governments were eager to press ahead.

In early September, the EDC Council of Ministers held its inaugural meeting in Luxembourg under the presidency of Konrad Adenauer. It then settled its internal organization and heard a report from Jean Monnet on the first steps taken by the ECSC High Authority. Later the same day, Robert Schuman and Alcide de Gasperi put forward a novel joint proposal.

Article 10 of the EDC treaty called for further steps toward political union to be prepared by the future EDC Assembly; but why wait, asked Schuman and de Gasperi, for the EDC treaty to be ratified? Why not request the ECSC Assembly, which was due to hold its own inaugural meeting in Strasbourg the following day, to recruit a few active members from France, Germany and Italy – to improve the balance of nationalities – and itself draw up plans for the political union? After some discussion, the council agreed on September 11.

Two days later, the Common Assembly in Strasbourg elected as President Paul-Henri Spaak of Belgium. After hearing and debating reports from Monnet and Adenauer, it turned to the Schuman-de Gasperi proposal to anticipate the work of the future EDC Assembly. Some opposed the plan as a slight to national parliaments which still had to debate the EDC treaty. Michel Debré – later to become President de Gaulle's Prime Minister – stipulated that he was 'favourable to a European political authority' nevertheless this 'authority must have a confederal character.' Eventually, however, the Common Assembly approved the proposal 58 to 4 with two abstentions.

The enlarged assembly, known as the 'Ad Hoc Assembly' held its first meeting on September 15. It worked fast. Within six months, by March 1953, it had produced a draft treaty for the European Political Community (EPC). This provided for a European executive council, to be known as the 'Ministers of the European Community,' a council of national ministers; a court of justice; and a parliament comprising a senate, whose member were to be chosen by the national parliaments and a people's chamber to be directly elected by the Community's citizens. Within two years, the ECSC and the EDC institutions would merge with those of the EPC but without abrogating their respective powers.

The EPC was to coordinate foreign policy, prepare a general common market for all goods and guarantee constitutional order and democracy within any member nation, either at its own request or on a unanimous vote of the council. But even on paper this ambitious construction had serious flaws. On the proposed common market, for instance, the EPC draft treaty was far less explicit than the later Rome treaty – itself an outline treaty establishing the European Economic Community.

But we will never know how the EPC could have coped with the constitutional crisis that arose in France in May 1958 or with dramatic events ten years later. The foreign ministers, meeting in later 1953, appointed a committee to work out fresh proposals. But the prospects for the EPC and its parent project, the EDC were already darkening.

The coal and steel treaty had taken a year to ratify in all six national parliaments. The debate had been tense. EDC, involving a European army, was even more controversial. In Germany, the Social Democrats opposed it as they had opposed the coal and steel plan. They argued that to integrate the Federal Republic with western Europe might block German reunification; its leader, Kurt Schumacher, was still more fearful of rearming his compatriots.

Only in March 1953, ten months after signing the EDC treaty did the Bundestag vote for its ratification. The Dutch and Belgian parliaments followed the next year as did Luxembourg. Nevertheless, two years after the treaty was signed, two parliaments still had not voted: Italy and France. In both countries opposition was growing. One reason was the thawing of the 'cold war', That year Stalin had died and the Korean War had ended [*in an armistice*].

But it was from France, not Italy and from the extreme right as well as the communist left that most opposition came. In November 1953, Charles de Gaulle, leader of his party, poured scorn on 'this monstrous treaty' and the other 'supranational monstrosities'. He did not mention Monnet by name but referred to him as 'the Inspirer.' In 1940, de Gaulle declared, Monnet had wanted to 'integrate King George VI with President Lebrun'; in 1943 to 'integrate de Gaulle with Giraud.' Now he was trying to integrate Germany with France. 'Since victorious France has an army and defeated Germany has none; let us suppress the French army... It won't matter, anyway, because the "European Army" will be at the disposal of the American Commander-in-chief.'

De Gaulle's reference to American pressure was accurate, if unfair. Under the new presidency of Dwight Eisenhower, the secretary of state was Monnet's friend, John Foster Dulles, whose championship of EDC was almost embarrassingly warm. Soon he would threaten an 'agonizing reappraisal' if EDC were to fail.

Dulles was a strong believer in European unity long before the EDC debate. He had spoken in New York in 1947 in favor of European unification, an action which captured considerable press attention since he was serving as foreign policy advisor to Governor Thomas E. Dewey, the leading Republican presidential contender. Dulles also showed his interest in a united Europe and his friendship for Monnet by cabling him in February 1953 that he was sending David Bruce, Monnet's old colleague from Paris, to head the US delegation to the Coal and Steel Community. (JMM, 379-80)

Monnet could not ignore this onslaught. He was interviewed in November by *Le Monde* and made short work of de Gaulle's nebulous proposals:

> They're out-of-date notions. They completely ignore practical experience which has shown the impossibility of solving Europe's problems by... full national sovereignty. What is this Confederation he proposes? If it is to have real power, the States will have to give it part of their sovereignty. If it has no powers, then it'll be just one more illusion.

But if de Gaulle's proposal were unconstructive, his negative influence was strong. Partly under his pressure, the French government promised they would not seek to ratify EDC until assured that Britain would be associated with it. At length, Britain made her offer but it was short of French hopes. Had EDC been put to the vote in France then, it might have succeeded. But delay followed delay; the French government fell, replaced by a coalition led by the Merlin-like Pierre Mendès France.

Paul-Henri Spaak, the Belgian Foreign Minister, was particularly anxious. He proposed a meeting of the Six. Germany and Italy accepted but Mendès France had too many other urgent worries. After Spaak met with Mendès France, his anxiety increased. Four of the Community countries had ratified EDC. Were they to await some unspecific amendments from France and then start the parliamentary process all over? The United States was pressing for a decision. Dulles had warned that further delay might cut military aid.

There was now talk of simply admitting Germany to NATO – a solution Spaak would prefer to EDC being turned into a simple coalition of separate European states. But the Six should at least hear and discuss Mendès France's counter proposals, he thought.

In July 1954, Mendès France secured an armistice in Indochina, one of his major distractions. When he expounded his proposals in Brussels with his partners, Mendès France undertook to secure a vote on them before year's end. He hoped the vote would be favourable but there was no chance of that on the EDC as it stood. His partners protested. All had seen forecasts and some had assurances that France could secure a pro-EDC majority if given a sufficient lead. What France was now asking, they argued, was that they should go back to their parliaments and with just as little certainty of success.

Shortly after, Spaak proposed a last-minute compromise but by now Mendès France seemed to have hardened his heart. He put the original EDC treaty before the National Assembly in a deliberately non-committal speech. EDC opponents then attacked it savagely – none with more emotion that Edouard Herriot, once the champion of European unity. Two days later, the Assembly rejected the treaty on a procedural motion by 319-264 with 43 abstentions. Mendès France and six cabinet colleague abstained.

When the High Authority's officials returned from their summer holidays in early September 1954, they were understandably gloomy. With the failure of EDC, the proposed Political Community had collapsed. Now the ECSC might collapse too. As one American observer put it, the ECSC 'was no longer the advance guard of a strong movement toward integration; it was more like an isolated outpost [...].' Almost simultaneously, the streets of Rome were crowded for the funeral of Alcide de Gasperi. To many, it looked as if the post-war unification of Europe was coming to an end.

For Jean Monnet, the rejection of EDC was a serious blow. 'Every day,' he said years afterwards, 'we could see the results. It didn't prevent the building of Europe but it certainly slowed it down.' To an English interviewer, he confided 'I was annoyed and – I don't like the word but I was pretty mad... Mad at myself because I was the one who had proposed to the French government... the acceptance of this European army. But it was not the end of the road.'

What was astonishing, in fact, to those who did not know Monnet, was how quickly he recovered. Not only did he continue to force the pace at the High Authority and to press forward the association with Britain. He also began planning how to relaunch the 'European idea.'

Two days after the French Assembly vote, he met in Paris with leading politicians. This was the beginning of many meetings throughout late 1954 and Spring 1955. In all Monnet made 21 trips to Paris; he went twice to Bonn, Brussels and Strasbourg and once to Metz. On those visits, or in Luxembourg he saw statesmen and officials from all Community countries.

In the midst of this activity, two months after EDC failed, Monnet took a decision which at first dismayed his friends. He announced to the High Authority that he would not seek re-election when his term ended in February 1955. The reason, he declared was 'in order to take part with complete freedom of action and speech in the construction of European unity.' Looking back, he explained

> I couldn't stay in Luxembourg which was essentially concerned with coal and steel. Europe is more than that; it must be. And so I resigned [but] also because I thought it was necessary to work for Europe from outside... I could only continue to have any influence on Europe... by leaving the High Authority.

But what should the action be? Monnet's young English associate, François Duchêne, suggested that Monnet might stand for election in the French Assembly to form a 'European' party in France. If this idea ever tempted him, he quickly changed his mind. More appropriate was to try to form a 'European' party on a European, not merely a French basis. As the idea took shape, Monnet came to think of it as a 'European Front' or action group, not of individuals but of the political parties and trade unions themselves.

Such a group must clearly have a programme. As the winter wore on Monnet and his friends worked on a number of drafts. They proposed action in four main fields. First, that the scope of the Coal and Steel Community expand to promote integration in energy and transport. Second, that the Common Assembly be directly elected. Third, that a new Ad Hoc Assembly be formed to prepare further steps toward unity. Fourth, that a new community deal with nuclear energy for peaceful ends.

Nuclear power – more so perhaps then at any time for a further 20 years – seemed to symbolize limitless possibilities. Monnet, after years at the Plan and the High Authority, was concerned with energy problems as such but he too felt the power of the atom. He made nuclear energy a central part of the proposed 'European Front.'

Early the next year, Pierre Mendès France's cabinet, already four times shuffled, now finally fell. The immediate result was to cancel the meeting to appoint Monnet's successor. He wrote from Luxembourg to the heads of the Six offering to stay on as long as necessary until his replacement was chosen. A second consequence was that Monnet now no longer had so suitable an occasion to make his intended speech. But this was a minor matter since what had begun as a draft speech had already turned into the plan for an action group.

He continued and intensified his efforts and prepared another set of drafts. In March 1955 he sent Jacques Van Helmont, who had worked with Spaak at the ECSC Assembly, to Brussels to show his former chief the new texts. The most important innovation was Monnet's suggestion that the whole project be considered by the community's Foreign Ministers.

Spaak now wrote the other Foreign Ministers for a meeting

> to relaunch the European idea by extending […] the Coal and Steel Community to all fields of energy and transport [and] […] peaceful development of atomic energy. An international conference [should] examine the idea and also the drafting of a treaty. Chairman of this conference could be M. Monnet.

Monnet discussed these ideas with Carl Friedrich Orphüls, now head of European affairs at the German foreign ministry. As Pierre Uri later described their conversation:

> Monnet was sure the Germans would be delighted to be accepted as equals in the nuclear field. To his great surprise, Orphüls told him the proposal would not be accepted by Germany.

Monnet realized, after further talks, that German reservations about atomic cooperation alone would disappear if wider economic integration was proposed. By Uri's recollection, it was then that Monnet and he put forward the idea of a general common market for all goods alongside the atomic community.

In fact, Uri's draft was one of a number circulating. A common market for all goods had already figured among the tasks proposed for the Political Community. Most recently, the Dutch Foreign Minister, Johan Beyen, had sent Spaak a plan for successive integration of various sectors of the economy.

As things turned out, both Uri's and Beyen's drafts played their part in the final outcome; Uri's more detailed work was crucial later on. But while he and Monnet debated these matters, problems arose in Paris. Their enthusiasm for the atomic plan was popular but lowering tariffs was not, exactly the opposite of Germany. Monnet's next few days were uneasy.

After further talks with Orphüls in Luxembourg, it was agreed that the foreign ministers would meet in Messina, Italy in late May. But the prospects were still clouded when Monnet went to Paris. From there he wrote to Franz Etzel: 'The situation is uncertain and confused. I myself don't know what to do. I sometimes wonder whether it wouldn't be preferable… to put off any action until later.'

But then the train of events Monnet had set in motion gave a further jolt forward. Beyen spoke in The Hague on his talks with Spaak and called for a study of general economic integration on supranational lines. Within 24 hours Monnet made a secret lightning visit to Spaak. The next day, Spaak was in The Hague where he and Beyen agreed to ask Joseph Bech of Luxembourg to join in submitting to the foreign ministers a Benelux memorandum.

From now on, Monnet kept in close touch with Spaak in late Spring 1955. When the Common Assembly met in Strasbourg, he had a call from Spaak: the reworked Benelux plan was on its way. With it came a covering note: 'Herewith your child.'

Monnet took advantage of the assembly session to confer with important allies, especially from France and Germany. On May 9, the fifth anniversary of the Schuman Declaration, he presented the High Authority's annual report and pointed out there was no contradiction between extending sector integration like atomic energy and pursuing general economic integration. The assembly voted a unanimous resolution calling for the foreign ministers to work toward 'the next stage of European integration.'

In mid-May Monnet paid another quick visit to Paris where he learned from Schuman, among others, of the French internal split on further integration. It was all the more vital, Monnet concluded, that Spaak and his colleagues should not be dissuaded from presenting the Benelux memo. It might initially embarrass the French prime minister, Edgar Faure, but with help from the 'Europeans' in his cabinet, it should surely tip the tables.

In Luxembourg two days later, Monnet received two crucial phone calls. The first from Spaak brought good news: The Benelux memo would be officially presented at the foreign ministers' conference. The second call was heavy with irony. It came from his old friend, René Mayer, who had just been proposed in Paris as Monnet's successor on the High Authority just as Monnet had been planning to withdraw his resignation.

In November 1954 when he first asked to be relieved of his duties, the prospects for Europe had looked bleak. Now they were hopeful – partly because of the incessant extra efforts Monnet had combined with his duties in Luxembourg. At the High Authority, he had resources – office, staff, drivers and telephone as well as an official platform. What was more, the Common Assembly which had urged him to reconsider his decision, voted two resolutions calling for the ECSC and Monnet himself to have an active role in 'relaunching of Europe.'

He then considered staying on. Mayer's call produced hesitation but not for long. Monnet sent off his letters to the Six governments and then to the press. "In the face of the relaunching of policy undertaken by governments, it would not be understood if I were not declaring myself ready once again to participate directly [...] should governments confirm the desire that several of them have insistently expressed to me.'

Was Monnet offering his services as High Authority president or for some task in the working out of the new steps in European integration on which the Messina foreign ministers' conference was to decide? Monnet's offer was rejected. The French cabinet chose René Mayer as France's candidate for the High Authority. But Monnet's actions may have had some effect. The same Cabinet meeting gave a broad mandate to Antoine Pinay, its delegate to Messina.

Monnet himself was in Paris over the three days surrounding the cabinet meeting where he congratulated Mayer. If he had any regrets, he suppressed them fairly quickly. For now the German government seemed to hesitate on the Benelux memo just when the French accepted it. A German paper tracked the Benelux plan but then seemed to question the need for institutional change. These views seemed close to those of Ludwig Erhard, Adenauer's stout, cigar-smoking economics minister who deeply distrusted both central planning and 'supranationality'. To have accepted these doubts, in Monnet's view, would have been fatal.

Monnet spent the next Sunday, Whitsun, at Bricherhof in his country house outside Luxembourg city, overlooking the sloping garden that ran down toward a beech wood valley. With him was Franz Etzel and they argued at great length about the German memo. Was all real progress about to be blocked? Etzel said the German paper had some merit: what had worked for coal and steel might not work for global economic integration.

Much later Monnet saw his way out of this dilemma. The High Authority, in fact, seldom behaved like a 'supranational government'. Its essential attribute was its independence rather than its direct power. When it acted on its own, it was within the rules prescribed in detail in the treaty; outside those limits, it acted in harness – in 'dialogue' as Monnet was later to call it, with the Council of Ministers. This was the model to be adopted later by the European Economic Community (EEC).

None of this, however, had been fully thought out in May 1955. Monnet and Etzel parted rather inconclusively. Etzel went to argue the case in Bonn, followed soon by a letter Monnet sent him by car. In it he repeated, very firmly and explicitly, his objections to the German memo. He agreed on the objectives, 'but absolutely not on the means of achieving them.'

On June 1 1955, the foreign ministers gathered at a former monastery in Taormina, Sicily, and later that afternoon drove some 25 miles along the coast to Messina. Their host was Gaetano Martino, Italian foreign minister and rector of Messina University; their chairman was the avuncular Joseph Bech. First the Benelux ministers explained their memorandum. To the surprise of some, Antoine Pinay approved it in principle although pointing out its many problems.

The Messina conference, before discussing its resolution, had quickly dispatched another item on the agenda. After some demur by the Germans, the ministers confirmed René Mayer to succeed Monnet at the High Authority. One chapter was opening, another was closing.

When the conference broke up on June 3 it voted a resolution several pages long but based principally on the Benelux plan. Expansion of trade, and freedom from tariffs and duties in a European market, harmonization of social regulations were all essential. Preparatory work toward a treaty would begin. The United Kingdom would be invited to take part. A report of a committee, chaired by a 'political personality', will be given to the ministers by October.

'Isn't it all very vague?' asked a journalist. 'No' said a spokesman, 'proposing a statesman to run it is a guarantee that it will work.' Soon afterwards, Paul-Henri Spaak was chosen to chair the committee which held its first meeting in Brussels on July 9 and worked thereafter on the Brussels outskirts at the Chateau de Val Duchesse. Its report, later than scheduled, went to the ministers in April 1956. Meeting in Venice the next month the ministers adopted it and turned the Spaak Committee into a treaty-making conference.

Within a year it produced treaties establishing the European Atomic Energy Community (Euratom) and the European Economic Community (EEC) or the Common Market. On March 25 1957 the two treaties were signed in the huge, ornate and crowded Sala degli Orazi a Curliazi on the Capitoline Hill in Rome. They came into force on January 1, 1958. The 'relaunching of Europe' was complete.

Officially it had begun with the Messina resolution but this in turn had been largely the result of Jean Monnet's ceaseless efforts during the nine months that had elapsed since the defeat of EDC. Like all his efforts, it had been partly collective and when made public, he took a back seat.

In early June 1955, Monnet made his farewells to the High Authority staff. Max Kohnstamm gave a buffet dinner for him. They stayed up talking to 2 am. The following week he noted in his diaries: 'I gave Uri a surprise – I tidy up my last papers.' Then he left Luxembourg for Paris.

The following week saw him in Scotland, staying with Cecil Weir. He wrote in his diary 'I try to catch salmon in stream without success.' He went on to Glasgow to receive an honorary degree. Ten days later he was honoured in his native town of Cognac in the presence of a thousand people – 'all Cognac'– as he noted. Not everyone realized he was more than the former head of the French Plan and the ex-President of the High Authority. Some knew he had instigated the Schuman Declaration but very few were aware of his role in the Pleven Plan and now the 'relaunching of Europe.'

The summer of 1955 had marked the diminuendo of Monnet's career. He was now 66. Many a man of that age, with so much achievement behind him, would have contemplated honorable retirement. Not so Jean Monnet.

IX. Sage

'All that I have to contribute is the experience we have had. In the face of an insoluble problem, you have to change the conditions and terms in which it is posed.'

To the end of his long life, Monnet still worried about problems, argued, inquired, invented, prodded and advised. He tired more easily and travelled rather less; but his brain was still disconcertingly sharp and it was still true, as Max Kohnstamm once said of him, that 'there isn't a statesman in the free world who doesn't listen' to what Monnet had to say.

Now, quite often, they came to seek him out. On December 18 1972, James Reston of the New York Times wrote:

> When Henry Kissinger was in Paris, he had a talk… with Jean Monnet. Ever since Colonel House and Harry Hopkins, White House aides have been turning to [Monnet] for help and while they don't always take his advice, he always has something sensible to say.
> Monnet, now 84, still going to his office every day, still living in his thatched-roof cottage here at Houjarray in the rolling countryside west of Paris, still taking his daily walk in the Forest of Rambouillet, and still looking optimistically toward the future.
> The problems of the nations change but Monnet's approach to them seldom varies. After a long walk through the forest, his cheeks were as red as his grandson's and his eyes as bright. He wonders why the Kissingers still come to see him since, he observes with a smile, 'I always say the same thing,' which is true. But what he says is the simple wisdom of a long and disciplined life of careful observation.

Reston had become one of Monnet's best friends. According to François Fontaine, collaborator on the Mémoires, *four of Monnet's five closest friends were Americans. Besides Reston, they were George Ball, David Bruce and John Foster Dulles. The fifth was Frenchman Etienne Hirsch.*

No one who knows Monnet would dispute Reston's summary, but Monnet himself has always added a rider. Speaking in September 1952 at the first meeting of the ECSC's Common Assembly, he had declared

> The tragic events through which we have lived…have perhaps made us wise. But men pass, and others will come to take our place. What we shall be able to leave to them will not be our personal experiences which will perish with us; what we can leave are institutions.

The phrase 'the United States of Europe', like most political slogans, had the double advantage of being at once spirited and imprecise. It offered verbal shelter to both the federalist lion and the internationalist lamb. It had already been used in the title of Monnet's speeches in the years 1952-54, *Les Etats-Unis d'Europe ont commencé*, which his High Authority colleagues had presented to him in 1956 shortly after the Messina Conference. Perhaps it lent itself to facile or forbidding analogies with the USA. But at least the expression dramatized the need to build real unity in Europe rather than set up weak intergovernmental organizations or form evanescent alliances.

The Action Committee for the United States of Europe (ACUSE), which Monnet had set up in 1955, met irregularly about once a year. An anonymous observer, writing in the Dutch publication, *Common Market*, aptly described it as 'something like the collective democratic conscience of the European Community.'

At one of its meetings, the committee discussed a draft declaration painstakingly prepared by Monnet and his small staff in Paris at 81 Avenue Foch, chief among them Max Kohnstamm and Jacques Van Helmont, assisted at different times by François Duchêne, myself, Pierre Uri, François Fontaine of the EEC's Paris office and a few others. Each draft normally began with rough outlines produced from talks between Monnet, his staff and delegates to the committee. These in turn were discussed and revised with the help of long research and studies going far beyond what appeared in the text itself.

One draft, at a particularly difficult time in Europe's development when all avenues seemed to be blocked, went through 140 versions over many months. At length a text emerged which was judged fit for distribution to the committee. Monnet and his colleagues then intensified the series of talks that had been proceeding on their travels round the capitals.

Committee delegates meanwhile sent written comments and amendments to Avenue Foch. By the time the committee met – usually for a two-day session – there was normally a broad consensus on what was to be decided. But this never precluded searching and sometimes heated debate which might lead to a complete revision or even replacement of the existing text.

During the night, if agreement had been reached on the first day, the final text was typed, translated and duplicated by Monnet's staff which included four secretaries and encompassed four nationalities and five languages. All Monnet secretaries were permanently overworked; on one occasion, a girl eight months pregnant stayed on for the all-night stint. Despite the pressure and the occasional rows, they stayed with him over the years, enhancing the family atmosphere in which he worked best.

On the following morning, the committee usually held its final meeting and presented its decisions to the press. By then, they had become the official policy of the member organizations.

Throughout this whole process, Monnet's role was crucial. Arguing, cajoling, intervening with suggestions, gently cutting short a fruitless debate or dissolving some apparently insoluble problem, he usually gave a remarkable and partly unwitting display of committee technique. His chairmanship made a bizarre contrast with his small figures and sometimes inaudible voice. What impressed and persuaded his hearers was his persistence, his patience, his seriousness, his good humour and the quick intelligence of his reactions. He always seemed ready to return to a point of detail if it involved a principle – or to accept a major change at a moment's notice if he thought he had been wrong.

Coupled with his exhaustive preparations during the previous months, including exploring almost all the objections and complication that could conceivably arise, Monnet's skill as a chairman usually enabled the committee to agree unanimously not only among different nationalities – which is relatively easy – but even between political opponents of the same country.

I personally shall never forget the Action Committee's Berlin meeting in 1965. It was the 20th anniversary of Nazi Germany's capitulation – which made this gathering of former enemies moving in itself. The Christian-Democrat Ludwig Erhard, by now Federal Chancellor, had come to pay his respects to the committee. Vast and curiously boyish, he sat next to the center of the top table. Two places away sat Willy Brandt, Social Democratic (SPD) leader and mayor of West Berlin, his face much bruised by life. Little more than a dozen years earlier, the SPD had been bitterly hostile to Monnet's plans for uniting Europe and Erhard himself had been highly critical.

Now they were reconciled – with their European partners, and, on this occasion, in the cause of Europe, with each other. And between the two Germans, small, serious, insignificant-looking, sat the patient architect of reconciliation, Jean Monnet.

***

The Action committee was not Monnet's only means of political pressure after he left the High Authority. The Monnet 'grape vine' of his friends and colleagues extended well beyond the committee. It included civil servants, businessmen and journalists as well as political and labour leaders, Americans as well as Europeans.

At key moments, however, the Action committee's work was especially effective in the first years of its existence, again in the mid-1960s during the political hiatus caused by the intransigence of General de Gaulle and in the lethargic 1970s when the Community needed another relaunch.

In October 1956, shortly after the Action Committee was set up, Monnet made a BBC broadcast. The rejection of the European Army, he declared, had been a serious blow to European unity. Pessimists had seen it as the end of all European plans. The establishment of the Action Committee was the proof that they were mistaken. The German Social-Democrats and some labour unions who had opposed the European Army now joined the Action Committee. Likewise, the French Socialists, for their part, had been deeply and publicly divided. Now they had publicly expressed unanimous support for the committee. The EDC quarrel was over.

The committee's first public success was to have its joint declaration on the powers and safeguard it sought for Euratom approved in all Community parliaments except Italy. When it met again in 1956, it was able to note that the Spaak Committee had produced its report (whose co-author was Pierre Uri of Monnet's staff) and that the Six foreign ministers had decided to convene a treaty-making conference which was already beginning work in Brussels.

It met again in September 1956. By this time, circumstances had changed. The Suez crisis and President Nasser's blockade of the Suez Canal had thrown into sharp relief Europe's dependence on imported oil. As the Action Committee pointed out, in words that were to seem prophetic decades later:

> The events of this summer have revealed that only a United Europe can make its voice heard, and be respected, in the world of today [...] by developing and uniting their resources, our countries can produce atomic energy [...] to keep their oil and coal imports within reasonable limits.

Jean Monnet, and the majority of the Action Committee, in no way sought a military solution to the Suez crisis such as was soon to be attempted by Britain, France and Israel. The committee recommended that Euratom and the Common Market treaties be concluded and ratified to come into force by 1957. In this timing they were disappointed. Furthermore, while France accepted that Euratom was exclusively for peaceful purposes, national nuclear defence programs should be allowed, it said, to continue alongside it.

In November 1956, in a resounding testimonial to Monnet's and his committee's influence, the Community member governments appointed Louis Armand, Franz Etzel and Francesco Giordani to present 'A Target for Euratom.' Armand, volatile, energetic and very French, contrasted piquantly with Etzel, the cool German lawyer and economist as they both did with Giordani, a thick-spectacled, bearded figure who looked like the 19th century layman's idea of a scientist. After a lightning tour of Western Europe, including the United Kingdom, and of Canada and the US, they presented their report in May 1957, six weeks after the signature of the two Rome Treaties.

After reviewing prospects for nuclear power, the warnings in the report on inaction on nuclear programs were largely ignored. By the next June, Armand himself had been president of the new Euratom Commission for six months when he had to admit that its target were likely to be deferred. Financial difficulties, new sources of oil and rising costs of nuclear power were to blame.

More immediately, Monnet's efforts and the report by the 'Wise Men' greatly helped secure ratification of Euratom and the Common Market. For him, this was an anxious and impatient time until the Six governments signed the Rome treaties.

The Action Committee held its fourth meeting to take stock. In his opening statement, Monnet was critical of the two years it had taken from Messina to treaty approval. The Committee pressed for the treaties' ratification by national parliaments. The German member agreed to seek an immediate Bundestag debate; France promised action before the summer recess.

France approved under a new government in July after a German vote gave overwhelmingly favorable approval. In the words of Professor Walter Yondorf, an American observer

> This episode shows that the Monnet Action Committee was sufficiently powerful to co-ordinate action between the France and West German parliaments and to hold its course in the face of a French government crisis.

Even before the two Communities formally began, Monnet was already concentrating on strengthening their institutions. In November, without holding a formal meeting, an Action Committee resolution called for

1. The grouping in the same place of the Institutions of the Coal and Steel Community, the Common Market [EEC] and Euratom.
2. The setting-up of the headquarters of the Institutions in a 'European District.'
3. The choice of a site easily accessible to all.

This proposal caused a flurry. The Luxembourg Christian Socialist Party disagreed, the first time that the Action Committee was not unanimous. Luxembourg was already conscious of the High Authority's busy presence and although the Action Committee refrained from suggesting a location, some Luxembourgers feared a further influx of foreigners. Monnet wondered whether Chantilly, north of Paris, might not be suitable.

At length Luxembourg changed its mind and indicated it would welcome the EEC and Euratom alongside the ECSC. By this time, however, it was too late. Brussels, a larger and more lively capital with better communications, was making a firm bid. Not for nothing had the treaty negotiations been concluded at its Château de Val Duchesse.

The Six Foreign Ministers met in early January. They appointed Walter Hallstein president of the EEC Commission; to head Euratom they named Louis Armand. But when they turned to siting the new institutions, they failed to agree on anything like the Action Committee plan. To avoid a stalemate, they finally agreed that the EEC and Euratom should meet in Brussels and Luxembourg, alternately.

Belgium took this as a defeat. Two major parties, the Christian-Socialists and the Socialists, both resigned [temporarily] from the committee. One of their members blamed Monnet for a 'purely French design.' The other said, with mild sarcasm, that he found Monnet 'above all a good Frenchman.'

If these members thought Monnet would not feel the wound, they were wrong. He wrote the Belgian members to review how the Brussels-Luxembourg compromise came about. The debate soon became academic. Although the EEC and Euratom were supposed to commute between the two sites, so much travel proved impracticable. Brussels soon became their de facto home. The High Authority remained in Luxembourg for some time together with the Court of Justice, now serving all three Communities. The Assembly, similarly enlarged, eventually assumed for itself the title 'European Parliament' and continued to meet in Strasbourg and increasingly Brussels but with its headquarters in Luxembourg. It was, and still is, an expensive and cumbersome compromise.

***

Rumours of a possible coup in France as a result of the Algerian War had been circulating for some weeks before the final drama of May 1958 which brought General de Gaulle back to power.

When he was asked to form a Government of National Safety and was voted into office, I, like several of my colleagues, felt relief for France but apprehension for Europe.

De Gaulle had favored 'a strategic and economic federation among France, Belgium. Luxemburg and the Netherlands... to which Britain might adhere.' Yet his followers had consistently opposed all European Community projects.

A passionately angry debate in the Common Assembly two years earlier now seemed more significant. Michel Debré – now to be de Gaulle's constitution-maker and later prime minister – had bitingly attacked the Spaak Report. Spaak and his committee, he said, had forced the Common Market and Euratom into 'the Procustean bed of ECSC institutions.' Then he had sat, white with fury, occasionally springing up to interrupt, as first Spaak, then others, had rounded on him with pulverizing force.

Even at the time, the spectacle had been disturbing. Those who recalled it now could not but feel nervous. They remembered, too, the no less passionate scorn that de Gaulle himself had poured on efforts at integration – to say nothing of his veiled attack on Jean Monnet.

Monnet's own feelings about de Gaulle had long been ambivalent. In 1940, he had rejected the idea of working with the General because 'he listens to nobody.' In 1943 he had helped preserve French unity by reconciling generals de Gaulle and Giraud but despite institutional safeguards this had ensured Giraud's defeat. Later, Monnet had served de Gaulle, first on the French Committee of National Liberation, then as founder and head of the French Plan.

In many respects, they were opposites: yet history drew them together and they baffled each other. Perhaps de Gaulle could never quite understand why Monnet was not a contender for power; while Monnet could never quite bring himself to believe that de Gaulle would not listen to reason.

Just after de Gaulle's return to power in June 1958, Monnet had a long talk with Cyrus Sulzberger of the New York Times. 'He could not mask his concern,' Sulzberger noted,

> about the possibility that de Gaulle would reverse the trend toward European integration. He had no doubt that Couve de Murville [now de Gaulle's Foreign Minister] is with us on basic policy. 'But', he added, 'de Gaulle is the boss. Much will depend on how long de Gaulle stays in power [...]. I am not too worried about what he has told you on European integration. De Gaulle's tactic has always been the same. He says no first; then he adjusts to yes later. Monnet thought de Gaulle the best solution for France's critical political problems. He added: He is an artist, an artist in power. He is not a dictator in the conventional sense of an organized party [...]. He wants to renew the bonds with the past, the ties he thinks have been destroyed. He had the greatest authority of anyone in France and can therefore solve the North African problem better than anyone else.

Most of Monnet's forecasts proved accurate. On the new constitution and on North Africa, de Gaulle fulfilled his expectations and Monnet voted 'yes' in the referenda of 1958 and 1961. On Europe, too, de Gaulle seemed to justify Monnet's guarded optimism for several years; in fact, the general's ideas and Monnet's observed a practical truce.

During this platonic honeymoon, Monnet and the Action Committee continued to encourage further development of European Community often along lines agreed with the presidents of the EEC and Euratom Commissions.

Monnet had known Walter Hallstein, President of the EEC Commission, since the days they had worked together on the Schuman Plan. Although the bookish, legalistic German bachelor was far removed in style and temperament from the buccaneering background of Jean Monnet, the two men shared deep convictions.

The atmosphere, in those early years of the Action Committee, was sometimes remarkably heady – perhaps even naïve – so much so that in the November 1959 joint declaration the committee already envisaged retiring from the scene. 'Today the Committee believes that the situation of our Six countries, as well as the common action [underway], should enable [...] European economic unity to be completed in the near future.'

The elegiac tone of this declaration may have owed something to the fact that Monnet had just celebrated his 71st birthday – one year beyond the Biblical span. But if he seriously imagined dissolving the Action Committee and perhaps retiring, the mood did not last long. Already, indeed, he had been moving into two policy areas where his ideas could hardly avoid a clash with General de Gaulle. The first was 'political union,' the second was the Community's relations with Britain and the rest of the world.

On political union, Monnet was a pragmatist. He tacitly agreed with Walter Hallstein that 'we're not in business – we're in politics.' But he would never have said, as Hallstein once did, that when economic union was achieved, political union would drop like a ripe apple from the tree. Monnet's position was clear in an earlier joint declaration of 1958: 'Today we can foresee the future political union of Europe. This unification is urgent. All major problems must be met on a world scale whether to avoid atomic war, the world population explosion or the economic situation.'

It was a sensible attitude. But Monnet was soon to be tempted out of it by the new 'European initiatives' from General de Gaulle. As the outline of an Algerian solution grew clearer, de Gaulle began once more to turn toward Europe. Provided that French interests, as he conceived them, were safeguarded, he now accepted the EEC but he was always uneasy in it, and hankered after something else.

De Gaulle wrote in his memoirs that he believed the unanimity required of the EEC Commission protected France. He also thought that regular meetings of the Six foreign ministers reporting back to their capitals would give their governments the final word.

With intergovernmental cooperation of this kind, unfettered by firmly agreed objectives, common rules and independent institutions, de Gaulle felt instinctively at home. A genuinely united Europe – the Treaty of Rome's 'ever closer union,' he later derided as an 'artificial motherland, the brainchild of technocrats.' 'My policy,' he wrote, 'aimed at the establishment of the concert of European States.' He then expanded this idea into a secretariat in Paris with elaborate proposals for 'organized cooperation between States.'

Jean Monnet had a fair idea, from private talks with de Gaulle's foreign minister, Couve de Murville, what was now in the wind. He raised the subject at the eighth meeting of Action Committee in 1960 whose declaration noted 'attempts... to further political unity. But there is still some uncertainly about the form political unification could take... The Committee is therefore convinced that progress towards political unity will be more quickly achieved as economic integration gathers momentum...' Clearly, suspicions were still deep.

Monnet himself was more hopeful. Although he had told Cyrus Sulzberger, in a further conversation in 1959, 'I have known de Gaulle for many years and I don't like him.' Monnet added: 'He has an odd technique. He always creates problems in order to solve them.'

With the general's scorn for European integration, Monnet's reaction was to persevere. But what should he do when faced with a proposal for top-level intergovernmental cooperation which might fatally weaken frail Community institutions he had laboured to set up? He might try to organize the rejection of de Gaulle's 'grand design', soldiering on with economic integration in spite of the furies such rejection might unleash. Or he might take the opposite risk by accepting de Gaulle's suspect proposals and trying to turn them into something more constructive.

Always an optimist, always ready to believe that others might listen to reason, and always convinced that unless one tries one can never be sure whether anything is foredoomed, Monnet now ranged himself for a time at least to make the best of the situation. As he described it to me long afterwards, 'One day I happened to meet de Gaulle. I suggested to him how he could become president of the European republic. He could announce a referendum, get himself elected for two years and then it would be Adenauer's turn.'

Monnet himself went so far as to draft a 'question to be put to a referendum in the Six community countries' on a European confederation. This would include, his draft stated, an executive whose decisions would be taken by qualified majority vote and a legislative body elected by direct universal suffrage. Existing EEC institutions would form an integral part of the confederation which was not to modify in any way the Rome treaties.

A month later, General de Gaulle gave more details of his own plan in a press conference. He prefaced them with further criticism of existing European institutions 'which do not and cannot have authority and political effectiveness.' Needed is a 'regular concert of the Governments responsible in each of the fields that are common and subordinate to Governments.'

There was enough in common between this and Monnet's ideas to make him feel that progress was possible but when he tried to win over his German friends he found them still shocked by de Gaulle attack on NATO and the existing communities. There was no point, they said, in ideological quarrels about federation or confederation providing existing institutions retained their powers. But de Gaulle's ideas were still very obscure.

Monnet did not give up hope. During three weeks in Autumn 1960 he wrote a long appeal to the Action Committee about the danger of complete inaction regarding the next steps to take. But the reaction was muted. He heard pleas from friends for the status quo yet he was fearful lest standing still should turn into sliding backward.

In November, Monnet sent a carefully worded letter to Konrad Adenauer. If anyone could launch the 'confederation' Monnet thought, it was the formidable German chancellor. He could, if he were determined enough, put 'European' substance into the airy proposals of de Gaulle. It was a last chance and it failed.

Three months later, in February 1961, the heads of the Six held a 'summit' in Paris. That night Adenauer dined with Monnet at Avenue Foch. The day's meetings had made progress but for Monnet the results were disappointing. There was to be no European referendum, the 'confederation' had been reduced to a plea for political cooperation with a secretariat, and an intergovernmental group of diplomats headed by Christian Fouchet who were to work out the ill-starred 'Fouchet Plan.'

The negotiations lasted many months. The diplomats worked on successive draft treaties submitted by France, counter-proposal from other countries, and a final attempt at compromise by Fouchet's successor, Attilio Cattani. It was a very far cry from Monnet's draft plan for a 'European confederation.'

Whether, as some suggested, the Fouchet plan might have avoided some of the later friction between the French and the other governments or whether as others feared it might have undermined community institutions, it remained hard to believe, with Monnet, that the institutions it proposed could really have contributed to greater unity on foreign policy and defence.

It was evident from a laconic ACUSE statement of 1961 that Monnet's early hopes were dimmed. The committee had never been enthusiastic about Fouchet. Besides, Monnet now had other urgent preoccupations.

***

What was essentially busying him by this time was the old question of Britain and her chance of joining the European Community after all. Monnet had always hoped that Britain would one day join as a full member rather than as an associate. He had hoped in 1955 that Britain might join the Action Committee. He even prepared a list of possible British members. But in the end the committee was formed without Britain just as the new communities were.

At the invitation of the Six, the British government sent an official to the Spaak Committee but had withdrawn him at the end of 1955. At that time there was no prospect of Britain accepting the discipline of the Common Market's outer tariffs. But in 1956 Britain began to toy with the notion of a Europe-wide free trade area in industrial products with no common outer tariff in which the community would be a member alongside other members of OEEC.

Later, many believed that the proposed free trade area would have dissolved the Common Market 'like a lump of sugar in a British cup of tea.' But Monnet and the Action Committee in 1956 called on governments to 'do all in their power to hasten [...] the Treaty for European Common Market and the completion of the OEEC studies for inclusion of the Common Market in a free trade area including the United Kingdom and other OEEC members.'

In January 1957 the OEEC produced a report on the complex problems involved. Shortly, the OEEC member states started work on them, first in expert committees, then in a full scale conference under the breezy chairmanship of Reginald Maudling who also headed the British negotiating team.

In its May 1957 resolution, the Action Committee continued to back the proposed free trade area. But late the next year Monnet wrote the committee that the free trade talks had been underway for nearly two years and 'the absence of results is leading to nervous tension both in our committee and in Great Britain.'

The following month, the free trade area negotiations were suspended after de Gaulle's minister of information bluntly announced that 'it is not possible to create the Free Trade Area as desired by the British [...] with no common outer tariff and no coordination of economic and social policies.'

The bitterness that resulted was acute. Nor was it confined to the British. In January 1959 Monnet had a long talk in Paris with Ludwig Erhard, who as the ultra-liberal German economics minister was a firm supporter of the Free Trade Area. Now, he was very angry with the Six. Monnet did his best to explain that the community in no way intended to form a 'bloc' to harm other countries. What the Six were doing was applying a method.

But there was an essential difference between this method and the principles of a free trade area. The Common Market had common institutions so as to take a common view and apply common policies, Monnet explained. The free trade area was an attempt to solve the problems among nations but without first trying to identify their common interests.

The Community, Monnet continued, must be open to Britain but it would not persuade Britain to join by giving up its fundamental principles. 'No one wants the British in Europe more than I do,' Monnet said. 'But we shan't have them in if we make too many concessions at the start.'

To calm the atmosphere created by the abrupt end of negotiations, the Community made a gesture extending to its OEEC partners some of trade concessions its member states were making to each other in a first step toward the full Common Market. What had annoyed Erhard was that some of the concessions had been extended precisely to stress the principle that the Six were forming an entity of their own.

The free trade area talks and their aftermath had raised fundamental questions about the Community's place in the world. One reason for Britain recently was that community countries now appeared to be discriminating against the rest of OEEC. Yet they were in reality forming a new collective entity and what was the

OEEC itself? It had been formed in response to Marshall Aid when Europe was destitute. Its separate members had been allowed to liberalize their mutual trade more rapidly than when they traded with the rest of the world.

In May 1959, Monnet left Paris for a week's talks in Washington. Then he returned to the United States the next month to discuss with Douglas Dillon, under-secretary of state for economic affairs, a paper 'A New Era of Atlantic Relations.' In July Monnet was able to discuss his paper – in which some American friends had a hand – again with Dillon.

Back in Europe he discussed it with Konrad Adenauer, with US ambassador to the EEC Jack Tuthill, and others. He sent a French translation to Antoine Pinay, de Gaulle's finance minister. Meanwhile events elsewhere in Europe moved rapidly. That summer Greece and Turkey requested 'association' with the EEC in default of the free trade area. Britain had been busy preparing to form the European Free Trade Association (EFTA) or 'outer seven' comprising herself, Austria, Denmark, Norway, Portugal, Sweden and Switzerland. By November the EFTA was ready for signature.

EFTA promised its members – aside from specific commercial advantages – three main purposes and one by-product. It discouraged other countries from following the Greek and Turkish example. It sought to prove that looser free trading worked and it appeared to strengthen its members as they pressed for a revival of the Maudling Free Trade Area. As a by-product, EFTA dramatized the division of Europe between the Six and the Seven which Britain took pains to point out to the US. The response, one American commentator said, was 'a coolness [that] [...] verged on hostility.'

Monnet and the Action Committee, as always, were anxious to 'change the context' of the dispute between the Six and the Seven. In November 1959, the committee approved a resolution that owed a great deal to Monnet's thought during the summer. It proposed that the EEC 'should hold a round-table meeting with Britain, the US and a non-Community country selected by the OEEC to seek a joint solution to what are from now on joint problems and [...] examine the permanent forms [...] for these consultations with other industrialized and under-developed countries while taking into account their differences.'

Despite misgivings by some ACUSE members, action followed quickly. The next month, Douglas Dillon spent a week in Europe discussing problems in major capitals. A western 'summit' proposed a special economic conference to be held in January 1960 in Paris. From it all emerged two main results. First, OEEC was reorganized as the Organization for Economic Cooperation and Development (OECD) dropping European from its title; second, a new Atlantic body – the Development Aid Committee – was set up, with and later, in it, to coordinate such aid.

Britain now began to reappraise her European policy, a task made a little easier for Harold Macmillan's government had now an increased majority. But the move took courage and imagination. In January, the British Foreign Secretary Selwyn Lloyd, took a first step at the Council of Europe's assembly with a review of British policy. 'I believe,' he said, 'we made a mistake in not taking part in the negotiations... which led to the Coal and Steel Community.' This was the public announcement; in London a special steering committee was set up for a confidential, high-level review. When completed, it concluded Britain should join the Community if it could.

In March Macmillan visited Washington where a leak to the *Washington Post* of some of his confidential musings indicated that the 'special relationship' was now being eclipsed by that arising between the US and the European Community. A further incentive came in May when the Community agreed to accelerate internal tariff cuts and move toward a common tariff with the rest of the world.

Jean Monnet was encouraged by the sense of movement but not by the partial approach by Britain to simply reconsider joining Euratom and ECSC. He said in a television interview in London that

'Coal and Steel, Euratom, Common Market' are all steps toward 'the main question [of] whether [she] will join the whole procession [...] and not a piece of it, leaving the rest aside.'

In July when ACUSE met in Paris, it underlined the same point with the hope

> that the United Kingdom and the other European countries will simultaneously become members [of the Communities] which are three facets of the same reality. The emerging European economic union is paving the way for a political unity, the exact nature of which cannot now be foreseen.

A further encouraging sign came in September 1960 when Edward Heath, who had joined Macmillan's government, addressed the Council of Europe Assembly: 'Why, you may ask, cannot the United Kingdom join the Community as it stands? In our studies we have maintained an open and flexible attitude to all solutions.'

Monnet kept a close watch on all these developments. The same month he sent aide François Duchêne to London for two weeks to sound out the views of civil servants, lobbyists, journalists and Commonwealth diplomats. He reported back that

> British attitudes have certainly much evolved [...]. Still the problems remain considerable and behind the officials' insistence [...] one often senses a hesitation [...] about participation in the Common Market [...]. In official circles in London there is still a tendency to see [...] relations with the Community as a trial of strength that is hoped this time will not be lost.

'One must expect,' Duchêne added, 'a fairly slow evolution of British policy.' Slow the evolution might be but Monnet was determined to assist it. He had studies made of the Commonwealth problems and he sounded out expert opinion in Brussels, again by Duchêne.

A February 1961 EFTA communiqué hinted about negotiations with EEC countries but full British membership in the Communities was more and more what Monnet had in mind. During the same Spring, he spent two days in London with Duchêne and Max Kohnstamm, meeting with influential friends. A brief, drafted by Duchêne with Monnet's close scrutiny, showed the direction of his thought:

> The UK must be a member of the Common Market on the same terms as France and Germany [...]. Trade problems raised by EFTA and by the French-speaking countries of Africa can be solved in normal negotiations.

To tackle these problems, Monnet and Duchêne sketched out some suggestions but Monnet's chief concern was to limit negotiations to a few key issues. 'The British always want to negotiate,' he once said, 'and the assumption in Britain [...] was that the entry into the Community would entail a substantial and lengthy process of bargaining partly concerned with amendments to the Treaties of Paris and Rome. Crudely summarized, the British attitude was "Negotiate now, join later."'

Monnet had already toyed with the opposite approach. 'Join now, negotiate from within.' That April he asked Jacques Van Helmont, his former and future assistant, then serving as a Community official in Brussels, how far Britain's problem could be solved by simply applying the treaties as they stood. Could Britain merely sign the treaties, adjusting their institutional provisions to secure a seat on the Council, etc. and deal with questions of substance afterwards through the normal workings of the institutional machinery? With a few exceptions, Van Helmont thought that this might be possible.

The advantages of such an approach were obvious. Speed was vital. No one knew how de Gaulle would respond to a British bid for membership but it would be hard even for him to refuse a request to join the Community unconditionally. The longer any negotiation continued, the more protests might arise for breaking it off. The longer Britain delayed, moreover, the more questions of substance the Community might settle in ways that would not suit British needs.

What scope was there, in any case, for substantial amendment to the treaties? On these, every government and parliament had a veto and most had great resistance to change.

Britain, it was true, faced notable difficulties. She had responsibilities toward the Commonwealth and toward EFTA. So would the Community, once Britain was a member. Already the EEC had responsibilities as the world's biggest trading power. If British entry would involve upheaval, there was no question of her entering without a transitional period. The more quickly she entered, the fewer adjustments would be needed.

Monnet recognized also the political problems. The British could make no move before consulting the Commonwealth and EFTA partners. British public opinion could not have understood 'Join first, negotiate later.' which would have been decried as a 'leap in the dark' or 'signing a blank check.'

He was uneasy when Macmillan made a statement in the House of Commons in April 1961 on the need for 'exploration' and 'clarification.' Soon after, a Monnet staff member wrote: 'While she appears to be preparing to join the Community, Britain [...] seems to intend taking a course that will certainly lead to failure.'

Throughout the next two weeks, Monnet had long discussions with Duchêne, Kohnstamm and Pierre Uri to isolate key questions that would have to be agreed, leaving others to be dealt with from within. His aim was whether and how 'Britain can join the Common Market by signing a very small number of clauses which raise no negotiating difficulties, the solution to substantive problems then being entrusted [...] to the Rome Treaty.'

The difficulties to such a procedure were not all on the British side. Within the existing Community, some suggested that British interests might be just as well served if she were to enhance association rather than seek full membership. When Monnet heard this idea in a speech of the German Foreign Minister Heinrich von Brentano, he wrote him:

> [Your speech] suggests it is possible to find a "middle path" which would be open to Britain and which would solve the problem of future relations with the Common Market. We have agreed for many years [that] Britain's full participation [...] [is] essential for the future of the West as a whole. [F]rom the very first in 1950 that was our aim [...]. But [...] we were convinced that British participation would only be possible once the British realized that Europe was on the road to success [...]. That day has come.

With Von Brentano, Monnet alluded to what became a persistent and often public element of British attitudes toward the Community: a desire for 'separation' from roles accepted by all other members. This tendency crippled the entire history of Britain in Europe and culminated in its decision in 2016 to withdraw from the EU.

A related question was how Monnet, and his British interlocutors, addressed the fact that membership in the Community meant a commitment to 'ever closer union' as the Rome Treaty stated and that this meant political integration. Monnet and ACUSE sometimes hinted at this problem but it became clear, over the following decades, that British interest in joining the Communities was only an economic matter.

In July 1961, Monnet was at Houjarray when a British embassy official brought a private message from Edward Heath: the prime minister was to announce the next day that the government was seeking to see if Britain could join the Community. Heath added a personal note to Monnet: 'We are very grateful for the efforts Monsieur Monnet has made to smooth our path and are confident that we can count on his help in overcoming the many difficulties that remain to be solved.'

Monnet replied immediately: 'I am deeply moved and much honoured' he said, 'by your message… I will do all on my part to smooth ways toward Great Britain joining the effort, both economic and political, to create the unity of Europe… I personally hope and I believe possible and important that the negotiations… can be concluded quickly.'

On July 11 1961, Harold Macmillan declared 'No British government could join the European Economic Community [...] without meeting the needs of the Commonwealth countries, the EFTA partners and of British agriculture [...]. [T]he ultimate decision whether or not to join depends of the results of the negotiations.'

For Monnet, Macmillan's speech made bitter-sweet reading. Although in a press statement that day he expressed his customary optimism, he was more guarded in a memo to the French foreign minister that same day:

> Britain's decision to join uniting Europe is one of the turning points in postwar war history [...]. The Prime Minister's statement [...] leaves some gaps which could later create grave difficulties. It appeared to aim only at the Common Market, not at the other Communities or at the "political union" at which the Six were aiming.

Monnet's immediate concern was to help the negotiations to a rapid conclusion. 'It is a mistake,' he told Agence France Presse in August, 'to think that large-scale negotiations are necessary [...]. What counts is to decide to see these questions [...] as a future construction, not of maintaining the past.'

That month the British government won its vote in the House of Commons. The same day Monnet wrote the Action Committee that the decision

> was the culmination of the policy we have constantly followed for the last ten years. However, some people are thinking and saying that Britain, once inside the European

institutions, will quite naturally put a brake on the development of Europe. I do not think so. I believe it will be quite the contrary [...]. Britain will be an active and constructive element.

Monnet went on to remind his colleagues of the Bonn communiqué affirming hopes that new Community members would assume the same responsibilities and goals of the original Six. He feared that 'technical problems' might obstruct the British negotiations. But he never seemed to face the problem that Britain wanted and sought only economic, not political, goals in its move toward Europe. Neither Monnet nor Mayne ever fully address this problem.

Before Edward Heath was to address the Six at a special meeting in Paris in early October, Monnet took the opportunity for a visit to London. He was anxious to persuade his British friends that 'a crucial choice' faced all of them. In summary, he noted:

> that either they may seek to disguise the changes involved... or the Six may feel that the Common Market is being undermined. Then Britain may feel that a wedge has been driven between her and the Commonwealth. Instead we recognize that Britain's entry, by broadening...the movement toward unity in Europe, provides an unprecedented opportunity toward an association of Europe and America.

In a lunch with Monnet, Harold Macmillan found him 'full of vigour as ever':

> He is very hopeful about the... negotiations and thinks that de Gaulle has changed his view... I had to tell Monnet that I thought the difficulties here were growing – pressure from Canada and Australia, anxiety of farmers, trade union fear of competition etc. I therefore hope we could have quick negotiations and get it over. Monnet agreed with this.

But if Monnet was 'very hopeful' that Sunday, a few days later he was uneasy again. When Heath made his statement, he said much that was reassuring: 'In saying we wish to join the EEC, we mean we desire to become full, whole-hearted and active members... in the widest sense and to go forward with you in the building of a new Europe.'

But the detail of the statement was less encouraging. It seemed concerned above all to perpetuate the economic and commercial patterns that were crystallized in the Commonwealth and the EFTA. What it appeared to envisage was not so much Britain's joining the European Community, as the Community joining with Britain in a vast free-trading system embracing...Western Europe, nearly all of Africa, and all the rest of the Commonwealth – discrimination on the grand scale against the United States, Latin America, Japan and the world's less developed countries.

Monnet used the month-long interval before the Brussels talks *[on British entry]* started to prevent them from entering 'a blind alley.' He presented the British ambassador to the talks with a 'strictly confidential' memorandum. It stated that 'The negotiations must be [...] radically simplified [by distinguishing] the broad decisions before Britain enters from the detailed working of those decisions' after entry.

The situation looked promising. Monnet was on good terms with the British and with the Americans, eager but silent observers of these events. He was in touch with Couve de Murville who as yet seemed to have no demolition orders [from de Gaulle.] The Action Committee comprised the majority political parties in all community countries except France. The head of the French team, at civil servant level, was his friend, Bernard Clappier.

But the key figure remained the British government. Would it accept leaving a large number of problems unsolved and questions unanswered at the time of its entry? The answer was No. Britain's official strategy remained exploratory negotiations, to see if the problems could be solved before formally deciding to join. Instead of lasting nine months or so, as Monnet had originally hoped, the negotiations dragged on for nearly fourteen before they were abruptly suspended by de Gaulle.

Not all issues had been dealt with by the time de Gaulle wielded his veto but the prospects for ultimate success were good – and for the general, perhaps, too good. Had Monnet's proposed procedure been adopted at the start, the talks might have succeeded before de Gaulle could readily have used his veto. True he might have halted them at any time; but he might have held back if they had made better progress before his settlement in Algeria or before Macmillan's agreement, in December 1962, to buy US Polaris missiles.

The bizarre details of the entry talks played into the general's hands: railway sleepers and kangaroo tail soup seemed a long way from the European idea. As it was his initial warnings proved unhappily right.

All this could only be guessed by Autumn 1961. When Monnet's suggestions were ignored, he was disappointed but not discouraged. A little against his better judgment, Monnet now departed from holding fast to principles, essentials, and procedures and became deeply involved in the technical debates about specific problems.

He flitted like a conspirator between Paris, Brussels, London and sometimes Washington. He never seemed to appear in the conference rooms in the Belgian foreign office in Brussels but he was often at his favorite old-fashioned Hotel Astoria there. Once, walking past the frosted glass door of the senior official who led the community negotiators, I saw a familiar shadowy silhouette in a dumpy overcoat and a trilby hat at times he seemed to be ubiquitous.

In mid-May 1962, both Max Kohnstamm and François Duchêne separately reported to Monnet disquieting news. Duchêne noted general pessimism in Brussels and quoted Clappier asking why the British were being so slow. The real difficulty, Kohnstamm said, 'is not that there is too little time, but too much.' Duchêne returned to Avenue Foch after lunching with a friend at the British embassy who was convinced that General de Gaulle would firmly oppose British entry.

On May 15, de Gaulle held one of his olympian press conferences. Championing his 'Europe of the States' as the only real Europe, he denounced anything else as 'myths, fictions and pageants'; He also hinted that the only 'federator' of Europe would be the United States and this for its own purposes; and he made another of his many attacks on NATO. But still de Gaulle had not come out against British entry. The negotiations continued.

Monnet spent his holiday that year in Switzerland, near Schuls in the Canton des Grisons. From there he suggested to Heath that they might meet in early September. But toward the end of August, he received further disturbing news. When Adenauer visited Paris in July, he had a secret meeting with de Gaulle, attended by only a few advisers. The chancellor expressed serious misgivings about the effects of British entry into the Community, addressing a number of technical problems. At this de Gaulle had risen to his feet. 'The time has come, Monsieur le Chancelier, to make an alliance between our two countries.' Adenauer had formally agreed. This was the germ of the Franco-German Treaty of Friendship signed in January 1963. It boded ill for mutual confidence within the Community – to say nothing of the prospects for Britain.

In early September, Monnet and Kohnstamm went to London where they learned from senior civil servants that Britain was now willing to concentrate on the most essential problem in the hope of concluding talks by year's end. But outside events intervened.

Both the US-Soviet crisis over Cuban missiles and the Skybolt missile dispute between the UK and the US, by demonstrating the power of the United States, increased both de Gaulle's determination to be independent and his distrust of the British.

That Autumn in Brussels was gloomy. Day after day the negotiations wrangled over complex problems. Then, for a while, hope revived. At a ministerial meeting in December, a committee was agreed to study rival proposals on agriculture being proposed by Britain and the Six. One week later the Action Committee met and referred to the Cuba missile crisis: 'Force may prevent war. It cannot create peace. To do so, the West must unite,' the committee continued, 'and prove that nothing could divide it.' This presupposed uniting Europe and building an equal partnership with the United States.

But it was not a question of agriculture that finally held up the negotiations; it was a long delayed answer from General de Gaulle; and that answer was No. On January 14 1963 he held his fateful press conference, then waited for the negotiations to stop. While in Brussels officials listened to his words on pocket transistor radios, their colleagues in the conference room worked on.

Two days later Couve de Murville formally requested an adjournment. For hours of bitter argument, the other five Foreign Ministers fought to keep the talks open. At length in late January, the delegations gathered once again where they had met for 15 months. One by one, they made final speeches. A German delegate sat weeping. Couve de Murville looked hunted and old.

Monnet came to Brussels during the final stages, joining in long discussions with the British and the other five. As he told Agence France Presse two days after the de Gaulle press conference, he still thought the negotiations could be concluded quickly.

The same day he wrote a long and heartfelt letter to Adenauer – the only man, he thought, who might be able to persuade de Gaulle to change his mind. Adenauer was due to visit Paris to sign the new friendship treaty.

The German Social Democratic opposition party wanted him to cancel the visit but the CDU/CSU and Free Democratic Coalition hoped Adenauer might take the opportunity to pressure de Gaulle and rescue the Brussels talks. Monnet shared this view and would normally have tried to see Adenauer during this Paris visit. But by unlucky coincidence, he was due to leave for Washington to receive the US Freedom Medal awarded him by President Kennedy.

Uncertain whether he could postpone his departure, he therefore wrote, in part, to the Chancellor:

> Our objective ever since the first day when I went to see you at the Schaumburg Palace in 1950, has always been to unite France and Germany, to link their destinies and to establish between their peoples a community of views [...]. I am well aware that you fear for the Community after the entry of Britain and a number of countries in her train. As regards Britain, I think her bearings must be fixed...if they are not, the direction of her future is uncertain. Britain [...] [is moved] to act today [because] they realize that their economic difficulties can no longer be solved in their national framework [...]. [I]f Britain is not part of the Community, Franco-German unity risks being very difficult to achieve.
>
> I think that [British entry] offers us an historic opportunity which we must seize. We shall then be [able] to start a partnership of equals with the United States and settle the problems of the common defence of the West.

He postponed his trip to America but whether or not his letter convinced Adenauer nothing would convince de Gaulle. Monnet told the AFP 'The failure [in Brussels] is very serious.' But he refused to believe it was the end of the road. He added: 'At this grave hour I think of 1954. Then, as now, the unity of Europe was momentarily halted and yet the necessity to unite finally forced aside all the obstacles. This will be the same today.'

For a while, Monnet was restless, casting around for ways to revive the issue. He and his associates worked at length and at speed to study how far they had got. More to the point were various plans then mooted – but not by Monnet – for 'interim' measures between Britain and the Six. One, known as the 'Spaak Plan,' was for an industrial customs union on items for which the British accepted the EEC's external tariff and an industrial free trade area on others. Monnet's chief reaction was fear it might attract British support.

General de Gaulle loftily suggested 'an agreement of association' – which seemed disquieting, unhelpful, or both. Monnet advised against it and was relieved when Heath condemned it roundly in the House of Commons.

In February 1963, Monnet had a talk with Couve de Murville – and was shocked. 'Since de Gaulle's veto, [he told Monnet] our Community had been paralyzed by his partners' refusal to concede anything to France's interests.' The French government policy was now to retaliate on a larger scale. 'The Six no longer exist,' he said. Instead, 'the Franco-German treaty will make possible such close cooperation… and a joint Franco-German viewpoint' [will] carry the day. 'The Four will follow and their attitude will be regarded as insignificant.'

It was urgent, thought Monnet, to stop the rot. As yet the Bundestag had not ratified the Franco-German treaty; one way to make it less harmful might be a preamble. He and his colleagues worked on a short draft that he took with him to Bonn. It declared:

> [T]he present Treaty will in no way affect […] the Treaties of Paris and Rome. Their objective will be to strengthen the Communities and to extend their scope. Consultations will be concerned […] with resumption of negotiations with a view to British membership […].

The Bundestag did not adopt Monnet's proposal. Instead, after a stormy debate but at length with near unanimity, it voted, in part, a simpler text of German goals of:

[T]he unification of Europe [...] traced by the European Communities, admitting to membership Great Britain and the other States that wish to join and the strengthening of the existing Communities.

But a preamble, however well-drafted, was small consolation for the wreck of so many hopes. Even decades later, it remains hard to exaggerate the dismay and confusion left by de Gaulle's veto. It was a blow to Britain because it postponed her hopes of joining the Community and ensured when she eventually did so [the EEC] would have made more progress and thus be harder to change.

It was a blow to the Community because it caused, as Walter Hallstein said, 'a constitutional crisis.' But most of all the veto seemed to shatter a vision – not a vision of Europe only, but a model for a desirable and attainable world organization. In its place, de Gaulle offered an ancient alternative: nationalism. Within the Community he had behaved with sudden, ruthless and implacable brutality, imposing his will without a word of consultation.

Earlier, in January 1962 President Kennedy had proposed 'an open partnership between the US and Europe.' He put forward a bill for a trade expansion act to negotiate reciprocal tariff cuts with the EEC. The bill was designed for an enlarged Community to include Britain. Five months later the Action Committee responded with one of its clearest and best declarations. Among other things it provided Monnet's most sophisticated and accurate description of how the Community worked:

> After trial and error, this method has developed into a regular interchange between a European body responsible for solutions to common problems, and the governments of members which put the national points of view.
> This is a completely new approach. It does not create a central government. But it does result in Community decisions taken within the Council of Ministers because [...] [it] makes possible, without risk, to give up the unanimity rule.

The Action Committee also defined the elusive notion of 'Atlantic partnership' of 'two separate but equally powerful entities [...]'. It was no coincidence that a few days later, on Independence Day 1962 that Kennedy made a 'declaration of interdependence' calling for 'equal partnership [...] [with] a strong and united Europe.'

Now it seemed that the fabric of that practical vision had been dissolved. Britain was excluded from the Community which itself was at a stalemate. One of its members seemed unwilling to contemplate partnership and the seeds of nationalism had once more been sown by France. Which country in Europe might reap them most dangerously was not hard to conjecture.

The year 1963, then, had begun badly but it continued worse. Before the year was over, Adenauer had retired and Robert Schuman had died; already the world had changed. Another who died that year was Pope John but still more tragic was the death in Dallas of President John F. Kennedy himself. It really seemed, by then, as if an epoch were coming to an end.

Throughout that year, Jean Monnet remained restless, spending long hours in reflection and discussion, making several speeches but uncertain where next to apply the lever of ideas. The Action Committee held no meeting: but all this time Monnet and his associates were working on a long declaration draft. Part of it concerned with the ideas on defence that Monnet had sketched in February. He and his colleagues had many meetings with military experts concerned with the 'Multilateral Force'. This American proposal, whose origins went back to the Eisenhower presidency, would establish 25 surface vessels, each equipped with missiles and manned by mixed crews from NATO members. Monnet saw it as a means of increasing transatlantic involvement.

Now Monnet worked out gradually – through over a hundred drafts – the elements of a system-built world. As it took shape, the text turned into a virtual Bible, a restatement and reassertion, of the truths that had been mocked. Finally, in June 1964, ACUSE met to consider it. Previously it had always met in Paris. This time it met in Bonn.

The declaration, then published with only minor alterations, seven abstentions and only one negative vote, specified 'the important and immediate steps' which the Committee believed could be taken toward these objectives:

To continue the unification of Europe;
To establish gradually equal partnership between United Europe and the United States;
To begin a joint policy in the nuclear field;
The action thus undertaken will make possible successive agreements [towards] peaceful coexistence between the West and the Soviet Union.

But in practice very few of the steps proposed were taken at the time. The value of this restatement of policy was shown the next year. In May 1965 Monnet convened another ACUSE meeting on the 20th anniversary of Hitler's defeat. What this meant to a German member was shown in his letter to Monnet:

May I thank you, for the great understanding you have always shown to my country. The meeting yesterday was a great success. Your voice, accompanied by [others] took the place of the French government which remained silent. We shall never forget what you have done for us.

On July 1 1965, the telephone rang on my desk at Avenue Foch. A Brussels operator asked for Monnet. He was standing beside me so I passed him the phone. He listened. 'Oui? Comment ça va? Comment?' On the line was President Hallstein of the EEC commission in great distress. France had failed to keep a deadline for agreeing on a farm finance solution. Couve de Murville, in the chair, had refused the traditional step to 'stop the clock,' had suspended the sitting and gone back to Paris.

What had happened was more complex than this story. Perhaps infected by the habit of package deals, the Commission had tied into one, three connected proposals: farm finance, Community budgeting and the European Parliament's increased role. France saw this as an attempt to buy institutional integration with hard cash. When France insisted on treating them separately by the previous deadline, the others wanted them together. France then boycotted the community institutions for seven months.

The Commission's proposed package was technically feasible but the political strategy behind it seemed rash. A few weeks before the crisis, I had lunched in Paris with a senior commission official and repeated to him remarks I heard attributed to de Gaulle. 'Once I have completed the common agricultural policy, I shall have no more to ask of the Common Market.' 'Exactly' explained my former colleague. 'That's why we must make him pay!' The idea of 'making de Gaulle' pay a measure of 'supranationality' for money that might have gone to France anyway seemed absurd. Monnet reproached himself for not advising against it.

In July Monnet met twice with Couve de Murville for lunch. The second time he noted that Couve was more hesitant; he recognized that the crisis was upsetting public opinion, including some industrialists and farmers and admitted that delay in settling it was harmful to everyone, including the French.

Monnet concluded that the general's intentions were still obscure. One might, therefore, fear the worst; so it was essential to end the crisis as soon as possible and above all, prevent community institutions from grinding to a stop. It would be criminal, he thought, not to compromise, as he wrote to Hallstein that month:

> In this shifting and uncertain situation, a fixed point must be Europe and the Common Market, with the institutions working again.
> We must solve this problem rapidly and in as 'narrow' a manner as possible. You ought to limit your proposal to the points agreed or nearly agreed to complete agricultural

markets and industrial customs union by 1967, to lay down financial regulation and to provide for independent [Community] financing by 1970.

Hallstein agreed but then, in September 1965, General de Gaulle held another press conference. Those who expected fireworks were not disappointed. The farm finance squabble, it now appeared, was of minor importance compared to majority voting. This de Gaulle rigorously rejected by making his by now predictable attacks on 'the very cumbrous international apparatus constructed at great expense around the Commission and often reduplicating the... Six governments.'

This seemed an attack on the European Community root and branch. This was confirmed the next month when Couve de Murville called for an 'overhaul' of the Community.

Monnet followed the crisis very closely, even again cancelling a trip to the United States, all the time counseling prudence. The Council [of Ministers] appealed to France to return. Some fiery spirits proposed the Five should invite Britain to fill France's empty chair; others, more fearful, wanted peace with France at any price. Monnet then issued a public statement hoping that France 'will make a positive response [...] to return to its place in Community institutions.'

Both appeals seemed to be in vain. In Brussels, however, the other Five remained firm. ACUSE could claim some responsibility for having ensured that the Germans, including the Foreign Minister Gerhard Schroeder, neither truckled to de Gaulle nor opposed his nationalism with nationalism of its own. The 'rappel à l'ordre' [call to order] of its Bonn meeting and its sequel in Berlin had been salutary, to say the least.

A presidential election was now approaching in France. De Gaulle was the obvious candidate but *Le Monde* asked if there would not be 'a European candidature?' There is no man in France as strong as de Gaulle,' the paper noted, 'but an idea may be as strong.'

These words of André Fontaine prompted *Der Spiegel*, the German news magazine, to wonder if Monnet might not be the 'European candidate.' He dismissed the idea with a chuckle but he was not neutral. Just before the election, in an unusual step, he issued a statement about his choice:

> Like many Frenchmen, I voted 'yes' to the 1958 Constitution, 'yes' to the election of the President of the Republic by universal suffrage, and 'yes' to the referendum on Algeria. On December 5 I shall not vote for General de Gaulle.

De Gaulle's opponent, Jean Lecanuet, whom Monnet supported, did not win but nor did General de Gaulle who obtained only 43%, not an overall majority. He was therefore forced into a run-off against François Mitterrand. Many believed that Lecanuet's vote, nearly 16%, was the principal cause of de Gaulle's decline. It was also clear that de Gaulle's creation of the crisis was one reason for his rather poor result.

On the eve of the second round, Monnet did his best to persuade friends to vote against de Gaulle, even if some distrusted Mitterrand. Monnet was more categorical: 'whatever the differences [between de Gaulle's opponents] Mitterrand has spoken out in favor of a Europe built by stages.' Monnet would therefore vote for him and he did.

General de Gaulle was re-elected but only just, by 55% of the vote. Following this relative rebuke, he finally agreed to return to the community institutions. The price was the 'Gentleman's Disagreement' completed in Luxembourg in early 1966. This involved some procedural concessions from France's partners but less drastic than those she had originally proposed. This 'Luxembourg Compromise' acknowledged what had always been the unwritten community law: it would avoid majority voting if a very important national interest was at stake.

Who had won? Neither side, fully. De Gaulle had suffered some humiliation; the 'Europeans' had been somewhat checked and made more cautious. The Commission had lost some prestige and privileges as well as some of its morale. Hallstein was later to leave his post. If there was any clear victor, it was the community system which had survived – however precariously – the most determined onslaught ever faced. Moreover, many had begun to question the 'European' credentials of General de Gaulle. For Monnet, the period following the 1965 crisis was a further interval of waiting. ACUSE was not to meet again until June 1967.

Meanwhile, de Gaulle's actions became steadily more extreme. He ousted Valéry Giscard d'Estaing from the finance ministry beginning a running battle between Gaullists and Giscard's Independent Republicans. In March 1966 he withdrew from NATO [institutions] though not from the Atlantic alliance. He insisted that all NATO units leave France.

In June he paid an inconclusive visit to Moscow. In August he went to Djibouti where a riot cancelled his speech and where early the next year a referendum voted for independence from France. In March the Gaullists lost 40 seats, scraping in with a bare majority. The next month the government started to rule by 'ordonnances.' A visit to Quebec where he cried 'Vive le Québec libre!' brought about his hasty departure. This preceded a verbal attack on Jewry and, in May 1968, student riots and industrial strikes.

In April 1969 came de Gaulle's defeat in his own referendum on regionalization and his abrupt withdrawal from power.

All this was in the future. In 1966, as he had done earlier, Monnet put his thoughts on paper. In a summer holiday, he wrote, in part, more for himself some vivid, if terse, sketches:

> Liberty means civilization.
> Civilization means rules and institutions;
> It is a privilege to be born in our civilization.
> Are we to limit these privileges behind national borders.
> Or are we to extend the privileges to others?
> We must maintain our civilization which is so much ahead
> of the rest of the world and organize [it] toward peace.

By Autumn 1966, his thoughts had been put into more formal shape. One draft, taken to Brussels, spoke of a European Political Community. It seemed sadly like whistling in the dark. But like many other drafts it was to undergo many changes before it saw the dawn.

Meanwhile, some encouraging signs came from Britain. Harold Wilson had enlarged his narrow 1964 Labour majority and, encouraged by Foreign Secretary George Brown, he began to reconsider Britain's stance with the Six. In January 1967 they began an exploratory tour of Europe covering Rome, Paris, Brussels, Bonn, The Hague and Luxembourg. 'By the time we finished,' Brown wrote in retirement, 'we had virtually decided to make our application.' After a great battle in the cabinet a majority voted to apply.

In March 1967, ACUSE announced a June meeting and supported themselves unanimously in favor of Britain's entry. The action, as everyone knew, did not include the Gaullists and in no way committed France. The next day Monnet gave an interview in *The* [London] *Times* urging full speed ahead. He attended the House of Commons debate called by Wilson. He was pleased with the all-party majority vote for the Motion although with some 40 Labour abstentions.

De Gaulle, two weeks later, held another press conference in which, without actually vetoing Britain's request, he dropped very broad hints. British entry, he said, would make a *tabula rasa* [blank slate] of the Community, a vast free trade area leading to an Atlantic area. Why not form an association? Or, better, wait until Britain had accomplished the 'profound economic and political transformation that is required?'

Monnet replied with a statement to the AFP: 'General de Gaulle admitted that the Community Six was a "prodigy" which must be preserved. Harold Wilson has agreed to join it. In what kind of society are we living if the Six are to reject without debate the request of a great democratic power to join Europe in the making?'

A summit meeting of the Six was to be held in Rome in June to mark ten years since the Rome treaty was signed. Monnet realized, of course, that de Gaulle still had a veto but he calculated that it would be harder… if negotiations were once allowed to begin. He therefore determined to use the authority of ACUSE in the most plangent possible way. It agreed to submit a series of resolutions for approval by the national parliaments. Concerning Britain one began: 'In response to the request for membership [by Britain] […] this Assembly declares itself in favour […] as it stands today, with the same rights and obligations of the Six'. *The Economist* commented that 'the Monnet Committee remains a potential power in Western Europe.'

In July 1967, British foreign secretary Brown, by a slight subterfuge, submitted his government's application to the Council of Ministers which, despite France's opposition, asked the Commission's opinion. Two months later, the Commission reported that, after exhaustive analysis, the talks ought to be opened.

Monnet and ACUSE worked to maintain and strengthen support for Britain. He wrote German Chancellor Kurt Kiesinger arguing that Britain's entry would help transform relations with the East. Monnet was there when the Bundestag debated the ACUSE resolutions. At one point, Kiesinger left the Chamber and minutes later he came back – but this time in the public gallery next to Monnet. It was a spectacular endorsement, followed by a unanimous vote for the principle of British entry.

The triumph did not last. In October France opposed the opening of negotiations. In November, de Gaulle in another press conference made French opposition definitive. For once, Monnet confessed himself discouraged. He said he was 'pessimistic'; France had denied the British 'that right essential to our civilization: that of being heard before being judged.'

But hope was kept up by the approval of the ACUSE resolution by the other Five. It sometimes seemed as if the medieval 'wheel of fortune' really existed for Jean Monnet, at the end of the nineteen-sixties. Within two years of his confession of failure, the whole situation changed.

The first change Monnet engineered himself by inviting British political parties and trade unions to join the Action Committee. He had feared the British would so annoy de Gaulle as to make further talks unthinkable. He finally overcame his scruples – judging no doubt that nothing would overcome his hostility now. Monnet now travelled many times between Paris and London. Party leaders, but not the trade unions, agreed to join.

Two days later further encouraging news came when the French Independent Republicans accepted his invitation to join ACUSE; Valéry Giscard d'Estaing would be one of its delegates. The ice seemed to be melting, even in France.

Before the committee could meet again, a French presidential election caused it to be postponed. On April 28 1969, having lost his last referendum, General de Gaulle issued a brief communiqué from his country home: 'I am ceasing to exercise my function [...] at midday today.'

With the election of Georges Pompidou to succeed de Gaulle, the reports of Monnet's experts lost something of their news value. But they were sound and imaginative in concluding that Britain's problems entering the Community could be solved. With two further sessions that year, ACUSE received the reports in Bonn and Brussels. In Paris, the political climate was changing.

At the December 1969 'summit', the Six began to open the door to Britain and other countries leading eventually to a lifting of what Pompidou at last admitted had been a further veto by de Gaulle.

Monnet's invitation to the 1970 Rome summit had been 'mislaid' but he was in Paris for the official commemoration on May 9 of the Schuman Declaration 20 years earlier.

By 1970, both Monnet and Mayne moved on to other tasks. Monnet was working with François Fontaine on his memoirs and Mayne on many writing projects including his unauthorized biography. Although Mayne's text does not cover the details, Britain was finally, in 1973, admitted to the European Community. In 1975, a referendum confirmed the matter when Harold Wilson's Labour government, which earlier, when in Opposition opposed entry, now supported it.

But it was on his 82nd birthday, on November 9 that year, that the de Gaulle period finally came to an end. Monnet was in London, discussing progress on the British talks which had formally opened in June by the new prime minister, Edward Heath. Late that day news came, General de Gaulle was dead.

Monnet once said that he disliked him. After watching a television broadcast, he turned to me and exclaimed: 'He's mad!' But these were passing reactions. Although de Gaulle thwarted so much of what Monnet stood for, I never felt he bore him a grudge.

Shortly after the general's retirement, I asked Monnet whether de Gaulle helped or hindered matters. He sat silent for a very long time. Then he said, 'I think both. I think... he developed the notion of the Community without Great Britain. But he also developed the notion of the Community and, at the same time, and in contradiction, the notion of France with her hands free.'

After de Gaulle's death, we had another talk on the subject, in French this time. 'Tell me,' I said, 'what was your reaction when you heard of his death? Myself, I was torn. I couldn't help feeling a certain regret.'

Monnet thought for a moment, then said reflectively, 'Ah, yes, he wasn't a great statesman but he was a great man. He found France in the abyss: he pulled her out...You know, I made a mistake. I ought to have talked with him, tried to convince him.' 'While he was out of office, you mean?' 'Yes, it was a mistake. I might perhaps have been able to convince him... But delegating authority – for him, that wasn't possible. For him, France was himself.'

Monnet then described his attempt to persuade de Gaulle to be voted president of the European republic. 'He called me and I explained the idea. He called in his staff. But he couldn't do it. When we were alone, he said to me "Would you like a more active life?" "I said," and here Monnet chuckled' "You know I'm only interested in one thing – Europe" And he said, "Yes, that's it. But he didn't do it. Perhaps I should have done[it]."' 'Do you think it might have worked? You sold him the Plan.' 'Maybe. But I don't think so.'

It remained hard to believe that Monnet could have had 'a more active life.' In the second, successful British talks, he played a less prominent part than in the earlier attempts. But he followed them closely as he followed their sequel and he was always prepared to offer helpful advice.

He was saddened to hear some of things said on the Labour side in the debates on the treaty of accession, just as he was when the party ceased paying its subscription to the Action Committee. He remained optimistic because he remained active, still inventing and perfecting and handing to the other men – for them to take the credit.

When Lyndon Johnson was President of the United States, Monnet put to him the counterpart of a Schuman Plan to reconcile Arabs and Israelis. Nothing came of it but it was typical of his concerns.

He helped shape, if not more, the practice of regular summits to smooth the path of Community institutions. He never retired. If he had not thought of doing so by the age of 86, when I was finishing this text, he seemed unlikely to change his ways.

***

'The Sage,' wrote a Chinese philosopher, 'is full of anxiety and indecision in undertaking anything, and so he is always successful.'

The first part of that was true of Monnet, as this account will have shown. It will also have shown that he was not always successful. What man is, except in political memoirs?

But the writers of triumphant memoirs may not be wrong. The question that counts in any man's life is: what has he achieved? In Monnet's case, the answer seems as simple as that of architect Christopher Wren. If you seek a monument, look around you.

I put this to Monnet obliquely, one Spring afternoon in Brussels. It was 1973, four months after the enlargement of the European Community which brought in Britain, Denmark and Ireland. The Action Committee was meeting in the huge steel, glass and concrete building that housed the Commission. As Monnet walked with me through the labyrinth, I gestured 'It's odd to think that all this was once a piece of paper on your desk.' Monnet's eyebrows rose. 'Yes, it's extraordinary.' Then, smiling, 'It's appalling.'

I knew what he meant. His friend, Bernard Clappier, once Robert Schuman's chief aide, told a British journalist: 'When I was much younger, I was mad about the European Community. As the years passed, I became less mad about it, and today I am not at all mad about it. But if the Community is a great deal less dynamic today than it used to be, it is also more solidly built than many people imagine.'

Anyone who remembers the makeshift urgency of revolution feels something of this when institutions take its place. I recalled what William Morris wrote in 1888, the year Jean Monnet was born:

> Men fight and lose the battle and the thing they fought for comes about in spite of their defeat, and when it comes it turns out to be not what they meant, and other men have to fight for what they meant under another name.

Institutions seldom live up to plans. Yet institutions, as Monnet had always insisted, are essential if what they stand for is to survive.

In Europe, what they and Monnet stood for is peace – not just between France and Germany – but gradually, starting with Europe as a building-block, extending peaceful dialogue to the beginning of an organized world. This is what Monnet always fought for; 'Europe' is a method even more than a place.

Monnet disclaimed personal tributes. By his own strict and generous lights, he was right to do so; all his efforts, he would argue, have been collective affairs. Other men deserve as much credit as he. But no one of a large group of old colleagues and friends who gathered once for one of his birthdays really agreed with him. They knew very well that without Monnet the collective efforts would certainly have been different, probably less effective, and possibly would never have been made, or made in time.

At the vortex of all those storms was the still centre of Monnet's deep moral intelligence; that, in the end is his secret. Not just charm and persuasiveness, not just energy, finally only flagging a bit at the end; not just persistence and patience, those old stubborn twins from the soil of Charente. Monnet had all these; but his really impressive virtue was his ability, in the midst of high drama or technical arguments of baffling complexity, to sit still, with his hands loosely joined on the table, and do what no one else present is truly doing: think.

✳✳✳

This was the end of Mayne's biography, except for the References. It was finished about 1974. Then he showed parts to Monnet with the drastic and negative reaction noted at the start [...]. About ten years after Monnet died in 1979, Mayne wrote a short appreciation titled 'Grey Eminence' in a book Jean Monnet: The Path to European Unity *(Douglas Brinkley and Clifford Hackett, eds, NY, 1991). Here, in part, are Mayne's final thoughts from that piece:*

To the end of his life, Monnet went on pursuing the goal of international peace. He was not always solemn about it. One day in London we were lunching at his favorite hotel. He had just succeeded in another effort at persuasion, this time involving the prime ministers of Britain and France. He was pleased and expansive. 'You know,' he said, 'the world we live in is very complex. We can't solve problems by tackling them head-on. We have to change their context. We have to find the point where a change can be made – a change that will go on by itself and change others things too.'

A waiter appeared. 'Would you care for a sweet, Sir?' 'Just a coffee,' we both said. 'Decaffeinated,' Monnet added. Another waiter brought a trolley full of truffles, gateaux, fruit salads and crème caramel. 'I'm tempted,' I said. 'So am I,' Monnet said. 'When you see them, it's different.'

Three other memories remain. At Monnet eightieth birthday party, friends from many countries gathered at Houjarray. I looked across the table at Monnet, sitting with Etienne Hirsch, his assistant and successor at the French Plan. Different as they were – Hirsch, the Jewish engineer, Monnet the Charentais entrepreneur – the two of them nonetheless looked like cousins: both short and compact, no longer young, both with clear, bright eyes, both smiling. Hirsch raised his glass, 'To Jean. Without him, some of us might not be here.'

Monnet's last political act was to publish his memoirs. At his request, I translated them. As I wrote, I could hear his voice in my head, virtually dictating the text. He was pleased with the outcome. Madame Monnet thought it 'more like Jean than the original.'

He asked me to go and see him in the familiar farmhouse sitting-room, surrounded by his wife's paintings. It was a quarter of a century since his first book, *Les Etats-Unis d'Europe ont commencé*, had helped persuade me to join his cause. Now Monnet was frail, and could no longer read but he talked as in the past. We both knew that we were saying goodbye. As I rose to leave, he took my hand in both of his – and then amazed me. 'Je vous donne ma bénédiction' he said.

Not long afterwards, on 20 March 1979, Monnet's family and friends gathered once more in a small country churchyard near his home. They came from at least two continents. The federal German chancellor had attended the funeral service as had the president of France. At first, the hymns and prayers had seemed incongruous, as if the Church were claiming Monnet for its own. His sister worked for the Catholic hierarchy and he had greatly admired Pope John; but, with colleagues at least, he had seldom spoken of God, or death or eternity.

Yet, on reflection, there was justice in the claim. What had been Monnet's secret? His wisdom? His patience? His great intelligence? His persuasive skill? Underlying them all, it seems to me, was something simpler and more mysterious: moral and spiritual strength. In the end, it was Monnet's goodness that made him unique.

Postscript

There were several indications that Mayne always wanted this biography published in some form:

1) Mayne was upset when Monnet accused him in 1975 of 'betrayal' for writing a full biography when he had originally intended only a short, popular work. Mayne agreed not to publish his text until the Memoires *appeared. By then the London publisher decided there was no market for a second large Monnet book. Mayne often and over several years, discussed his long text with the hope it might eventually be used. (Interviews with Mayne in my own book* Who Wrote the Memoirs of Jean Monnet? *(NY, 2016), 98-9 and FJME AMS 8/3/9-10)*

2) While describing the Monnet Memoires, *which he translated into English, he wrote to Monnet that he would have liked 'more physical details – how people looked, what they wore, what the food and weather were like. In my own unpublished work on the same subject, these fill out the details.' (FJME in its archives on the* Memoires *AMS 8/3/22)*

3) In his family-published autobiography The Copper Stick, *(Leistershire, UK, 2015, 182) Mayne reflected on his last conversation with Monnet (cited above, p. 215) The 'benediction' given by Monnet, Mayne now understood, meant that he had Monnet's approval for publication of a Monnet biography.*

4) Mayne's draft of a biography of Monnet, he wrote, was 'unpublishably long [...] [but] I actually thought it quite good.' (The Copper Stick, 200,281) He agreed in 1989 to review his manuscript for its 'nuggets. It is too long but needs no extensive rewriting.' (Personal conversation with Mayne)

5) Mayne gave the present editor his draft text in 1989 for reduction and editing. He also gave copies to François Duchêne and, indirectly, to an American historian, for possible use in their Monnet biographies. This indicates Mayne's strong desire to see his work used. (The Copper Stick, *182,200 and* Who Wrote the Memoirs of Jean Monnet? *76-7).*

An Historial Footnote on Brexit

Both François Duchêne and Richard Mayne were fervent believers in a United Kingdom as part of the European Union. These beliefs were reflected in their respective careers with Jean Monnet and in their written accounts of both his life and of their own outlooks. Neither anticipated (nor could probably have understood) the drastic decision in the 2016 referendum by their home country to leave the EU after over 40 years of membership, the step called Brexit.

Duchêne, in a rare criticism of Monnet in Jean Monnet: The First Statesman of Inter-dependence (W.W. Norton and Company, NY, 1994), *wrote that his mentor believed that Britain 'would be captured by its dynamic' after its 1973 entrance into the Community. His view 'could not have been more mistaken' Duchêne wrote (Duchêne, 381) after reviewing British attitudes toward Europe since 1950.*

Richard Mayne never made such an explicit judgment about Monnet's views on the British role in Europe but he once told me that one could not understand fully that role without reading Michael Charlton's book, The Price of Victory. *(See p. 135). That book presents a quite pessimistic account of Britain cautious and even half-hearted approach since 1950 to European integration. Mayne's respect for that analysis suggests he would have been appalled but perhaps not surprised entirely by the 2016 decision to leave Europe.*

References

Much of the material in this book is based on personal knowledge or private information. Written works consulted below are followed by chapter references where appropriate.

(These are Mayne's original references, minus some minor periodicals no longer available and with chapter references consolidated. He did not use footnotes because, he told me, much of the material was based on his own experiences with Monnet. Also, he was somewhat dismissive of frequent footnotes which he though interrupted the narrative. Ed)

General

Charlton, Michael, 'My Europe,' interview with Jean Monnet, *The Listener* (BBC) No. 2390, Jan 23 1975

Fontaine, François, in *Réalités*, December 1962

Fontaine, François, *Jean Monnet*, Lausanne, 1963

Mayne, Richard, *The Recovery of Europe*, London, NY, 1970, 1973

Mayne, Richard, 'The Role of Jean Monnet', *Government and Opposition*. No 3, 1967

Rieben, Henri, *Jean Monnet*, Lausanne, 1971

Rieben, Henri et al., *La Greffe européenne*, Lausanne, 1973

Suffert, Georges, 'L'Europe de Jean Monnet,' transcript of French television I broadcast, Sept 11, 1970

Time magazine, October 6, 1961

Watson, Alan, 'The Father of Europe,' transcript of BBC-I broadcast, November 31 1971

Weisenfeld, M, transcript of interview with Jean Monnet, German television, 1965

By Chapter (where appropriate)

Acheson, Dean, *Present at the Creation*, London, 1970 (VII, VIII)

Acheson, Dean, *Sketches from Life*, New York, l960 (VIII)

Action Committee for the United States of Europe, *Statuts de l'association de gestion administrative*, Paris, 1957 (VIII)

Action Committee for the United States of Europe, *Statements and Declarations, 1955-67*, London, 1969 (VIII)

Adenauer, Konrad, *Erinnerungen*, Frankfurt, 1967-70 (VIII)

Agar, Herbert, *A Time for Greatness*, London, 1943 (V)

Anouil, Gilles, *La Grande-Bretagne et la Communauté Européenne du Charbon et de l'Acier*, Issoudun, 1960, (VIII)

Armand, Louis, Etzel, Franz, and Giordani, Francesco, *A Target for Euratom*, Luxembourg and Brussels, 1957 (VIII)

Attlee papers lodged at the University College, Oxford (VIII)

Ball, George, *The Discipline of Power*, Boston, 1965

Bauchet, Pierre, *La Planification française*, Paris, 1966, (VI)

Beloff, Max, *The Intellectual in Politics*, New York, 1971 (IV)

Beloff, Max, *The United States and the Uniting of Europe*, London, 1963 (VIII)

Beloff, Nora, *The General Says No*, London, 1963 (VIII)

Benoit, Emile, *Europe at Sixes and Sevens*, New York, 1961 (VIII)

Birrenbach, Kurt, *Die Zukunft der Atlantischen Gemeinschaft*, Freiburg-in-Breisgau, 1962 (IX)

Bjol, Erling, *La France devant l'Europe*, Copenhagen, 1966 (VIII)

Bok, D.C., *The First Three Years of the Schuman Plan*, Princeton, 1955 (VIII)

Brandt, Willy, *A Peace Policy for Europe*, London, 1969 (IX)

British Labour Party, National Executive of, *European Unity*, 1950 (VIII)

Brooks, John, 'The Common Market,' *The New Yorker*, September 22 - 29, 1969 (IX)

Brown, George, *In My Way*, London, 1972 (IX)

Brugmans, Henri, *L'Idée européenne* 1918-56 (VIII)

Brugmans, Henri, *Le Message européen de Robert Schuman*, Lausanne, 1965 (VIII)

Bryant, Arthur, *Triumph in the West 1943-46*, London, 1965 (VI)

Bromberger, Serge & Merry, *Les Coulisses de l'Europe*, Paris, 1968

Bullitt, Orville H. (ed), *For the President: Personal and Secret, Correspondence between F.D. Roosevelt and William C. Bullitt*, London, 1973 (III)

Butcher, Harry C, *My Three Years with Eisenhower*, New York, 1946 (VI)

Calvocoressi, Peter, *Survey of International Affairs 1952*, Oxford, 1955 (VIII)

Camus, Albert, *Essais*, Paris, 1967 (VI)

Cadogan, Alexander, *Diaries 1938-45*, London, 1971 (IV)

Camps, Miriam, *Britain and the European Community 1955-63*, Oxford, 1964 (VIII)

Camps, Miriam, *European Unification in the Sixties*, New York, 1966 (IX)

Camps, Miriam, *What Kind of Europe*, London, 1965 (IX)

Carter, W. Hornfall, *Speaking European*, London, 1966, (VIII)

Catroux, Georges, *Dans la bataille de la Méditerranée*, Paris, 1949 (V)

Charpentier, Maryse, (ed) *Dossier de l'Europe des Six*, Paris, 1969 (VIII)

Churchill, Allen, *The Incredible Ivan Kreuger*, London, 1957 (III)

Churchill, Winston C., *The Second World War* (pbl ed) London, 1964

Churchill, Winston C., *The Sinews of Peace, Postwar Speeches*, London 1948 (VIII)

Colebrook, M.J, *Franco-British Relations and European Integration 1945-50* (II, VII)

Colvin, Ian, *Vansittart in Office*, London, 1956, (IV)

Crawley, Aidan, *de Gaulle*, London, 1969, (V, VI)

Cook, Don, *Floodtide in Europe*, New York, (VI, VII, VIII)

Council of Europe, Consultative Assembly, *Reports, 1950*, Strasbourg, 1950 (VIII)

Crozier, Brian, *De Gaulle*, London, 1973, (V, VI)

Dalton, Hugh, *High Tide and After: Memoirs 1945-60*, London, 1962 (VIII)

Dalton, Hugh, Papers, lodged at the London School of Economics (VIII)

Davenport, John, *Fortune* magazine, Aug 1944 (VI)

Davidson, Ian, *Britain and the Making of Europe*, London, 1973 (IX)

Davies, Pamela N. *The Origins of the European Coal and Steel Community*, Unpublished Ph.D. thesis, University of Reading, 1974 (VIII)

De Carmoy, Guy, in Waites, Neville, (ed.) *Troubled Neighbors*, London, 1971

De Gaulle, Charles, *Mémoires de guerre*, Paris, 1968, (V, VI)

Diebold, William, Jr., *The Schuman Plan*, New York, 1959 (VIII)

Diebold, William, Jr., *Trade and Payments in Western Europe*, New York, 1952 (VII)

Drouin, Pierre, *L'Europe du Marché commun*, Paris, 1963 (VIII)

Dulles, John Foster, *War or Peace*, New York, 1950

Dumaine, Jacques, *Quai d'Orsay* (1945-51) (VI)

Eden, Anthony, *Memoirs: Full Circle*, London, 1960

Elgey, Georgette, *La République des illusions 1945-51*, Paris, 1965 (VI, VIII)

Elgey, Georgette, *La République des Contradictions 1951-54*, Paris, 1968 (VIII)

Ellis, Howard S., *The Economics of Freedom*, New York, 1950 (V, VI)

European Coal and Steel Community, *Agreement; Correspondence between ECSC and United Kingdom*, Luxembourg, 1954 (VIII)

Fauvet, Jacques, *La IVe République*, Paris, 1959 (V, VI)

Flanner, Janet, *Paris Journal 1944-65*, London, 1966 (VI, VII, VIII, IX)

Folliot, Denise, (ed) *Documents on International Affairs, 1952, 1954*, Oxford, 1955, 1957 (VIII)

Fontaine, André, *Histoire de la guerre froide*, Paris, 1965-67 (VIII)

Fontaine, François, *La nation frein*, Paris, 1956, (VIII)

Fontaine, Pascal, *La Comité d'Action pour les Etats-Unis d'Europe de Jean Monnet*, Lausanne, 1974 (VIII, IX)

Fourastié, Jean & Courtheoux, J.-P, *La planification économique en France*, Paris, 1963 (VII)

Freedman, Max, (ed.) *Roosevelt and Frankfurter: Their Correspondence 1928-45*, London, 1970 (V, VI)

FRUS, 1939, Vol II Washington DC (IV)

FRUS, Europe, 1943, Washington DC (V)

Freymond, Jacques, *The Saar Conflict 1945-55*, London, New York, 1960 (VIII)

Furniss, Edgar S., Jr. *France, Troubled Ally*, New York, 1960

Gerbet, Pierre, in *La Revue française de science politique*, July-Sept 1965, (VIII)

Gillois, André, *Histoire secrète des Français à Londres de 1940 à 1944*, (V) Paris, 1973 (VI)

Giraud, Henri, *Mes évasions*, Paris, 1946 (V)

Giraud, Henri, *Un seul But, la victoire*, Paris, 1949 (V)

Gladwyn, Lord, *Memoirs*, London, 1972

Gouzy, J.P., *Les pionniers de l'Europe communautaire*, Lausanne, 1968 (VIII)

Graubard, Stepher H. (ed) *A New Europe?*, Boston, 1964

Griffiths, Richard, *Marshal Pétain*, London, 1970 (V, VI)

Grosser, Alfred, *La IVe République et sa politique extérieure*, Paris, 1961 (VIII)

Haas, Ernst B., *The Uniting of Europe*, Stanford, 1968 (VIII)

Hackett, John & Anne-Marie, *Economic Planning in France*, London, 1963 (VII)

Haight, John M., 'Roosevelt and the Aftermath of the Quarantine Speech,' *in Review of Politics* April 1962 (IV)

Haight, John M., 'France's First War Mission to the United States,' in the *Air Power Historian*, January 1964 (IV)

Haight, John M., *American Aid to France*, New York, 1970. (IV)

Hall, H. Duncan, *North American Supply*, London, 1955 (IV, V)

Hall, H. Duncan & Wrigley, C.C., *Studies in Overseas Supply*, London, 1956 (IV, V)

Hancock, W.K. and Gowing, M.M. *British War Economy*, London, 1949 (IV, V)

Hansard, House of Commons, February 21 1955, London, 1955 (VIII)

Harvey, Oliver, *Diplomatic Diaries 1937-40*, London, 1970 (IV)

Heiser, Hans Joachim, *British Policy with regard to the Unification Efforts on the European Continent*, Leyden, 1959 (VIII)

Hirsch, Etienne, in *Les Cahiers de la République*, Paris, January 1963

HMSO *Anglo-French Discussions*, May-June 1950, London, 1950 (VIII)

HMSO *Negotiations for a European Free Trade Area*, London, 1959 (VIII)

Hoffmann, Stanley et al, *France: Change and Tradition*, London, 1963

Huen-de Florentiis, G, *Robert Schuman*, Milan, 1964 (VIII)

Hull, Cordell, *Memoirs*, London, 1948 (V, VI)

Hunter, Leslie, *The Road to Brighton Pier*, London, 1959

Ismay, Lord, *Memoirs*, London, 1960

Jouve, Edmond, *Le Général de Gaulle et la construction de l'Europe (1940-66)*

Juin, Alphonse, *Mémoires*, Paris, 1959 (VI)

Kaspi, André, *La Mission de Jean Monnet à Alger mars-octobre 1943*, Paris, 1971 (V)

Kimball, Warren F., *The Most Unsordid Act: Lend-Lease 1939-41*, Baltimore, 1969 (V)

Kitzinger, Uwe, *Diplomacy and Persuasion*, London, 1973

Kitzinger, Uwe, *The Second Try: Labour and the EEC*, London, 1968 (VIII)

Kleiman, Robert, *Atlantic Crisis*, New York, 1964

Kohnstamm, Max, in *A new Europe?*, Boston, 1964 (VIII)

Kohnstamm, Max, *The European Community and its Role in the World*, Columbia, Missouri, 1964 (VIII)

Laurent, Jacques, *Année 40 - Londres - de Gaulle - Vichy*, Paris, 1965 (IV,V)

Leahy, William D., *I Was There*, New York, 1950, (V)

Lecerf, Jean, *Histoire de l'unité européenne*, Paris, 1965, Jan 1963

Ledre, C., *Robert Schuman*, Paris, 1964

Lemaigre-Dubreuil, Jacques, *Les relations franco-américaines et la politique des généraux*, Paris, 1949 (V)

Lerner, Daniel & Aron, Raymond, *France Defeats EDC*, New York, 1957 (VIII)

Lindberg, Leon N., & Scheingold, Stuart A., *Europe's Would-be Polity*, Englewood Cliffs, New Jersey, 1970 (VIII)

Ling, Cheng, H, *The Chinese Railway: A Historical Survey*, Shanghai, 1935 (III)

Lippmann, Walter, *Western Unity and the Common Market*, Boston, 1962 (VIII)

Lister, Louis, *Europe's Coal and Steel Community*, New York, 1960 (VIII)

MacLennan, Malcolm, *French Planning: some lessons for Britain*, London, 1961

Macmillan, Harold, *The Blast of War 1939-45*, London, 1967 (V)

Macmillan, Harold, *Tides of Fortune, 1945-55*, London, 1969 (VIII)

Macmillan, Harold, *At the End of the Day*, London, 1972

Mahotiere, Stuart de la, *Toward One Europe*, London, 1970

Maisondieu, J, *Jean Monnet et l'organisation de l'Europe*, Thesis at University of Paris, 1972

Malraux, André, *Les Chênes qu'on abat*, Paris, 1971

Mason, Henry L., *The European Coal and Steel Community*, The Hague, 1955

Massip, Roger, *Voici l'Europe*, Paris, 1958

Massip, Roger, *De Gaulle et l'Europe*, Paris, 1963, (VIII)

Maurois, André, *Memoirs 1885-1967*, London, 1970

Mayne, Richard, *The Community of Europe*, London, 1962

Mayne, Richard, *The Recovery of Europe*, London, New York 1970

Mayne, Richard, *The Institutions of the European Community*, London, 1968

Mellserts, G., *La genèse du Marché commun*, Lausanne, 1968

Mengin, Robert, *De Gaulle à Londres vu par un Français libre*, Paris, 1965 (V)

Meynaud, J. & Sidjanski, D., in *Annuaire Européen*, Vol XIII, 1965

Middleton, Drew, *The Defense of Western Europe*, New York, 1952

Moran, Lord, *Winston Churchill: The Struggle for Survival*, London, 1968

Moch, Jules, *Histoire de réarmement allemand depuis 1950*, Paris, 1965

Monnet, Jean, *Les Etats-Unis d'Europe ont commencé*, Paris, 1955 (VIII)

Monnet, Jean, *Allocution à Scy-Chazelles le 3 Octobre 1965*, Paris, 1965 (VIII)

Moore, Ben T., *NATO and the Future of Europe*, New York 1958

Mowat, R.C., *Creating the European Community*, London, 1973 (VIII)

Mulley, F.W., *The Politics of Western Defence*, London, 1962

Murphy, Robert, *Diplomat Among Warriors*, London, 1964 (V)

Newhouse, John, *Collision in Brussels*, London, 1968 (VIII)

Nicolson, Harold, *Diaries and Letters 1939-45*, London, 1967

Novick, Peter, *The Resistance versus Vichy*, London, 1968

North Atlantic Treaty Organization, *Documentation sur l'Organisation*, Paris, 1952

Northrup, F.S.C., *European Union and United States Foreign Policy*, New York, 1954 (VIII)

Nutting, Anthony, *Europe Will Not Wait*, London, 1960 (VIII)

Olivi, Bino, *L'Europe difficile*, Milan, 1964 (VIII)

Palmer, Michael et al, *European Unity*, London, 1968 (VIII)

Pendar, Kenneth W., *Adventure in Diplomacy*, New York, 1945 (V)

Pflimlin, Pierre A & Legrand-Lane, Raymond, *L'Europe communautaire*, Paris, 1966

Pierrard, Pierre, *Dictionnaire de la IIIe République*, Paris, 1968

Pinder, John, *Europe Against de Gaulle*, London, 1963

Pisani, Edgard et al, *Problems of British Entry into the EEC*, London, 1969

Pleven, René in Tournoux, Raymond, *Secret d'Etat, II: Pétain et de Gaulle*, Paris, 1964

Price, Harry Bayard, *The Marshall Plan and its Meaning*, Ithaca, NY, 1955 (VIII)

Prittie, Terence, *Adenauer: A Study in Fortitude*, London, 1971

Racine, Raymond, *Vers une Europe nouvelle par le Plan Schuman*, Neuchâtel, 1954 (VIII)

Reston, James, 'Jean Monnet on the Coming Year', *NY Herald Tribune*, Paris, December 18, 1972 (IX)

Rodens, Franz, *Konrad Adenauer*, Munich, Zurich, 1965

Rosenman, Samuel I., *Working with Roosevelt*, London, 1952

Rouanet, Pierre, *Mendès-France au pouvoir 1954-55*, Paris, 1965 (VIII)

Sahm, Ulrich, in Hallstein, W. & Schlochauer, H.-J., *Zur Integration Europas*, Karlsruhe, 1965

Salter, Arthur, *Allied Shipping Control*, Oxford, 1921 (II)

Salter, Arthur, *The United States of Europe*, London, 1933

Salter, Arthur, *Memoirs of a Public Servant*, London, 1961

Salter, Arthur, *Slave of the Lamp*, London, 1967

Sauvy, Alfred, *De Paul Reynaud à Charles de Gaulle*, Paris, 1972

Sayers, R.S. (ed.) *Banking in Western Europe*, Oxford, 1962

Schlesinger, Arthur M. Jr., *A Thousand Days*, Greenwich, Conn. 1967

Schmitt, Hans A., *The Path to European Union*, Baton Rouge, Louisiana, 1962

Schnurre, Wolfdietrich, *Berlin: Eine Stadt wird geteilt*, Freiburg im Breisgau, 1962

Schoenbrun, David, *As France Goes*, London, 1957 (VIII)

Schuman, Robert, *Pour l'Europe*, Paris, 1963 (VIII)

Sherwood, Robert E., *The White House Papers of Harry L Hopkins*, (Titled *Roosevelt and Hopkins* in USA) London, 1949 (IV, V)

Shirer, William L., *The Collapse of the Third Republic*, London, 1972

Siegfried, André, *De la IVe à la Ve République*, Paris, 1958

Smith, Howard K., *The State of Europe*, London, 1950

Soloveyilchik, George, *Ivar Kreuger*, London, 1933

Spaak, Paul-Henri, *Combat Inachevés*, Paris, 1969

Spanier, David, *Europe our Europe*, London, 1972

Spears, Edward, *Assignment to Catastrophe*, London, 1956 (IV, V)

Spears, Edward, *Two Men Who Saved France*, London, 1966 (IV)

Stehlin, Paul, *Retour à zéro*, Paris, 1968

Stettinius, Edward R. Jr., *Lend-Lease*, London, 1944 (VI)

Stimson, Henry L., & Bundy, McGeorge, *On Active Service in Peace and War*, New York, 1947

Sulzberger, C.L., *The Last of the Giants*, London, 1972

Taber, George N., *John F. Kennedy and a United Europe*, Bruges, 1969

Taylor, A.J.P., *English History 1914-45*, Oxford, 1965

Tournoux, J.-R, *La Tragédie du Général*, Paris, 1967

Uri, Pierre, *Partnership for Progress*, New York, 1963

Van der Beugel, Ernest H., *From Marshall Aid to Atlantic Partnership*, Amsterdam, 1966

Van der Goes van Naters, Marinus, *Le Développement de l'intégration économique*, Luxembourg, 1955

Warner, Geoffrey, in Waites, Neville (ed.) *Troubled Neighbors*, London, 1971 (VIII)

Watson, Alan, *Europe at Risk*, London, 1972 (IX)

Weiss, Louise, *Mémoires d'une Européenne*, Paris, 1969

Werth, Alexander, *France 1945-55*, London, 1956

Werth, Alexander, *The Strange History of Pierre Mendès-France*, London, 1957 (VIII)

White, Theodore H., *Fire in the Ashes*, New York, 1953

Williams, Philip M., *Crisis and Compromise: Politics in the Fourth Republic*, London, 1964

Willis, F. Roy, *France, Germany and the New Europe 1945-67*, London, 1965

Willkie, Wendell L. *One World*, London, 1943

Wilson, Harold, *The Labour Government 1964-70*, London, 1974 (IX)

Zaring, J.L., *Decision for Europe*, Baltimore, 1969

Zurcher, Arnold, *The Struggle to Unite Europe 1940-55*, New York, 1958 (VII, VIII)

Index

The father of Europe

The father of Europe

The father of Europe

Original Author

Richard Mayne was born in 1926 in London where he grew up until World War II moved his early school years to Berkshire. He continued his education at St. Paul's and Cambridge, the latter in several stages After a brief military career which included Egypt he returned to university where he began a career of writing for publication while studying history.

His interest in an integrating Europe brought him to Luxembourg where he worked in the emerging Coal and Steel Community. His work brought him to the attention of Jean Monnet in Paris in 1956. He worked twice for Monnet in the 1950s and 1960s, alternating with his boyhood friend, François Duchêne, as bilingual advisers.

His lifelong passion for the European Union informed his many roles in both working in and describing its growth. His work as journalist, historian, broadcaster and critic extended and widened his career. He wrote 13 other books and countless articles and reviews before his death in 2009 including an autobiography The Copper Stick.

Final Author and Editor

Clifford Hackett was born in 1930 in New Haven, Connecticut, USA. He began his formal education at St. Louis University with a degree in philosophy. He continued at Yale University with a degree in history. He served in Germany in the US Army and for ten years in Europe, Africa and Washington DC in the Foreign Service.

He worked for thirteen years in both Houses of Congress and then independently on international issues, especially European integration, as a consultant, editor and writer.

He is an historian who published Cautious Revolution: The European Community Arrives, NY, 1990, 1995 and edited Jean Monnet: The Path to European Unity (with Douglas Brinkley), NY, 1991. He edited and co-authored Monnet and the Americans 1995 and wrote A Jean Monnet Chronology, 2008, both published by the Jean Monnet Council, Washington DC, where he is executive director. In 2016 he wrote Who Wrote the Memoirs of Jean Monnet? NY. He lives in Berkeley Springs WV and Washington DC.

The Foundation was created in 1978 by Jean Monnet, the designer of the first European Community and the first honorary citizen of Europe. He entrusted all his archives to the Foundation. An independent institution serving the public interest, a non-partisan and a non-militant structure, the Foundation receives support from the State of Vaud, the Swiss Confederation and the City of Lausanne. It operates out of the Dorigny Farm, located in the heart of the campus of the University of Lausanne, its main partner.

Today the Foundation houses and exhibits many other private archives, notably those of Robert Marjolin and the European papers of Robert Schuman and Jacques Delors, as well as iconographic and audio-visual documents. It includes a specialized library and a European documentation centre. The Foundation collects testimony from key actors and witnesses as a part of its filmed interview programme. It thus provides users, and especially researchers, with a coherent corpus of documentary resources on the origins and development of European construction and on Switzerland-Europe relations. Every year, the Foundation awards its Henri Rieben Scholarship to several advanced PhD students.

Thanks to the internationally recognised importance of these collections and to the collaboration between Jean Monnet and Professor Henri Rieben, who chaired the Foundation until 2005, the Foundation has become a European intellectual crossroads and an essential venue for meetings, debates, and reflection about major current European issues. It regularly organises conferences, European dialogues, and international symposia, forming partnerships with prestigious institutions. It periodically awards its Gold Medal to prominent political figures who have worked for the common interest of Europeans; among the laureates are José Manuel Barroso, Emilio Colombo, Mario Draghi, Valéry Giscard d'Estaing, Jean-Claude Juncker, Helmut Kohl, Romano Prodi, Helmut Schmidt, Martin Schulz, Javier Solana, and Herman Van Rompuy. The Foundation also welcomes many visitors and researchers, who are given assistance in their work, in addition to contributing to the training of students. Thanks to support from the State of Vaud, the Foundation created a new activity in 2016, a "think tank" made up of a group of experts, currently working on sustainable mobility in Europe.

An editorial mission supplements the range of the Foundation's activities. The Red Books Collection, which was created by Henri Rieben in 1957, has been co-published with Economica since 2007 and now comprises 218 titles. A new series of shorter publications, the Debates and Documents Collection, was launched in 2014. These publications tend to highlight the Foundation's documentary collections, its public events, or the expertise of its members and partners.

Every year, the General Assembly of the Council of the Foundation – consisting of about 530 members from all walks of life – is held, as well as the Scientific Committee. Pat Cox, former president of the European Parliament and the European Movement International, has been the president of the Foundation since 1st January 2015. His predecessors are José Maria Gil-Robles (2009-2014), former president of the

European Parliament and the European Movement International; Bronisław Geremek (2006-2008), member of the European Parliament and former minister of Foreign Affairs of Poland; and Henri Rieben (1978-2005), professor at the University of Lausanne. Since 2012, the director of the Foundation has been Gilles Grin, doctor in international relations and lecturer at the University of Lausanne.

Issues that have already appeared in the series

Ferry, Jean-Marc: *Les voies de la relance européenne,* numéro 1, avril 2014, 51 pp.

Grin, Gilles: *Méthode communautaire et fédéralisme : le legs de Jean Monnet à travers ses archives,* numéro 2, septembre 2014, 27 pp.

Cox, Pat: *De la crise économique à une crise politique dans l'Union européenne?* numéro 3, septembre 2015, 59 pp.

Cox, Pat: *From Economic Crisis to Political Crisis in the European Union?,* issue 3, September 2015, 55 pp.

Gil-Robles, José Maria: *L'investiture de la Commission européenne : vers un gouvernement parlementaire pour l'Union européenne,* numéro 4, décembre 2015, 43 pp.

Dehousse, Renaud: *Quelle union politique en Europe?* Entretien réalisé par Hervé Bribosia, numéro 5, mai 2016, 51 pp.

Cox, Pat: *Europe after Brexit,* issue 6, July 2016, 27 pp.

Grin, Gilles: *Shaping Europe: The Path to European. Integration according to Jean Monnet,* issue 7, March 2017, 34 pp.

Martenet, Vincent: *Un pacte pour réformer et refonder l'Union européenne,* numéro 8, mars 2017, 54 pp.

Cox, Pat; Oliva, Patrick; Kaufmann, Vincent; Lundsgaard-Hansen, Niklaus; Audikana, Ander et Huberts, Leo: *Mobilité durable: Un appel aux décideurs européens,* numéro 9, mars 2018, 37 pp.

Cox, Pat; Oliva, Patrick; Kaufmann, Vincent; Lundsgaard-Hansen, Niklaus; Audikana, Ander and Huberts, Leo: *Sustainable Mobility: An Appeal to European Decision-Makers,* issue 9, March 2018, 37 pp.

Fontaine, Pascal: *La méthode communautaire: entretien réalisé par Chantal Tauxe,* numéro 10, novembre 2018, 33 pp.

Cox, Pat: *A European Parliament Election of Consequence,* issue 11, December 2018, 15 pp.

Cover: alain kissling / atelierk.org
Inner Layout: atelier Kinkin

Fondation Jean Monnet pour l'Europe
Ferme de Dorigny
CH - 1015 Lausanne
www.jean-monnet.ch

ISSN 2296-7710

9 772296 771001